Trap with a Green Fence

TRAP WITH A GREEN FENCE

Survival in Treblinka

RICHARD GLAZAR

Translated by Roslyn Theobald

NORTHWESTERN UNIVERSITY PRESS

Evanston, Illinois

Northwestern University Press
www.nupress.northwestern.edu

Originally published as *Die Falle mit dem grünen Zaun* by Fischer Verlag.
Copyright © 1992 by Richard Glazar. English translation copyright © 1995 by
Northwestern University Press. Published 1995.

Printed in the United States of America

10   9   8   7   6

ISBN-13: 978-0-8101-1169-1
ISBN-10: 0-8101-1169-1

Library of Congess Cataloging-in-Publication Data

Glazar, Richard, 1920–
    [Falle mit dem grünen Zaun. English]
    Trap with a green fence : survival in Treblinka / Richard Glazar ;
translated by Roslyn Theobald.
        p. cm. — (Jewish lives)
    ISBN 0-8101-1184-5 (cloth). — ISBN 0-8101-1169-1 (paper)
    1. Treblinka (Poland: Concentration camp) 2. Holocaust, Jewish
(1939–1945)—Poland—Personal narratives. 3. Glazar, Richard, 1920–. 4.
World War, 1939–1945—Atrocities. 5. World War, 1939–1945—Personal
narratives, Jewish. I. Title. II. Series.
D805.P7G5513 1995
940.53'18'092—dc20
[B]
                                                            95-6051
                                                                CIP

∞   The paper used in this publication meets the minimum requirements of the
American National Standard for Information Sciences—Permanence of Paper for
Printed Library Materials, ANSI Z39.48-1992.

❖

Contents

Foreword by Wolfgang Benz   *vii*

Sketch of the Treblinka Concentration Camp   *x*

Fouling the Stars with the Dust of the Earth   3

I Know How to Handle Cattle   5

That Much Fantasy   11

The Name "Treblinka"   15

My Next Pair of Pajamas   21

"*Eli, Eli*—They've Thrown Us into the Fire and the Flames"   29

Death's Secret Workshop   35

Ten for One   39

The Hangmen and the Gravediggers   45

A Little Something in Your Pocket   59

Typhus versus Plan H   69

Balkan Intermezzo   83

The Uniformed Riders of the Antichrist   99

The Key to the Munitions Depot   109

Masquerade   117

Camouflage   127

2 August 1943   137

On through Poland: A Little to the Left, and Then to the Right   147

Rhineland Steel and Rhineland Wine   163

Those Strange Chamber Pots on Their Heads   177

A Villa in One of the Finer Quarters   189

Penance Accompanied by Bassoon   195

❀

Foreword

Treblinka, acccording to one widely available reference work, was an extermination camp southeast of Warsaw that operated from 1942 to 1944: "A total of 900,000 people were put to death at Treblinka; mostly Jews, 323,000 of whom were from the Warsaw Ghetto. In 1943 approximately one thousand interned laborers took part in an uprising at the camp."

Much more could be said, and various points need correcting. First, the Treblinka death camp was not located southeast of Warsaw; it was northeast of Warsaw on the border of the "Generalgouvernement," that part of Polish territory that was occupied and governed by Germany during the war. The deadly machinery of Treblinka began operating on 23 July 1942. The inmate uprising on 2 August 1943 was part of the final phase of operations, the final two transports having arrived on 18 and 19 August 1942 (from the Białystok Ghetto). From the autumn of 1943 on, on orders given by the murderers in command, all activity in the camp centered on covering up all traces of its existence.

The vague and incorrect entry quoted above is only one indication of how little concrete knowledge about these terrible sites of organized murder is available today. It is also an indication of how much we have forgotten about the history of this camp, even including its geographic location.

We might well note here that the exterminations at Treblinka— unlike the murders in Auschwitz—were carried out with the exhaust from motors piped into rooms where thousands of people were herded together. In addition to the brutality of the SS and their Ukrainian accomplices, mechanical breakdowns occurred, when the motors stopped running and the half-dead victims were kept waiting while repairs were made. After Auschwitz-Birkenau, Treblinka was the largest site of industrial mass murder organized by the National Socialists.

Very few people survived Treblinka. Richard Glazar, one of the inmates who took part in the uprising of August 1943, wrote this account immediately after the end of the war, before his return to Prague. Because no publisher could be found for the Czech manuscript, it remained unpublished for more than four decades. In 1990 Glazar edited his original text, translated it into German for publication in Fischer Verlag's Jewish Life Series, and added a section on the intervening period of his life.

Richard Glazar was born into a Jewish-Bohemian family in Prague in 1920. His father had been an officer in the Austro-Hungarian army, and the family spoke both Czech and German. Until the German army marched into Czechoslovakia in 1939, the Glazar family's knowledge of anti-Semitism was based more on hearsay than on experience. The parents hid their nineteen-year-old son in an out-of-the-way village, and he lived there undiscovered until the summer of 1942. It was then that he fell into the hands of German occupation troops. He was taken first to the Theresienstadt Ghetto at the beginning of September, and then on to Treblinka at the beginning of October.

The hell of Treblinka lasted ten months for Richard Glazar. Escape through Poland, work as an alien laborer under an assumed identity back in the Reich, a life of constant threats from air raids and the liberators—the dangers appear to come to an end only upon his return to Prague in the summer of 1945. Of his family, besides himself, only his mother was still alive; she had survived both Auschwitz and Bergen-Belsen.

Following the war Richard studied in Prague, Paris, and London, earning a degree in economics. During the Stalinist era in Czechoslovakia he was considered "a politically unreliable element"; after the disintegration of the Prague Spring in 1968, he immigrated with his family to Switzerland, where he now lives.

In 1957 he returned to the town of Treblinka on a business trip. In 1963 and 1971, in Düsseldorf—at the trials of the Treblinka murderers and their accomplices—he was again confronted with his past, when he was called to testify about the murder of millions of Jews. Only fifty-four survivors had answered the summons to assist the courts in their search for justice.

Richard Glazar recorded his experiences immediately after the war and then did not talk about them again for many years. He sees his story as a legacy and a tribute to the reality of a genocide that is denied again and again by those who will not see, from whose perspective there is no firm proof (*stichhaltige Beweise*) of the existence of Auschwitz and Treblinka, Sobibór and Belźec.

WOLFGANG BENZ

Sketch of the Treblinka Concentration Camp

1-3 MAX BIALA BARRACKS

1   Living quarters for the (Ukrainian) SS guards
2   Living quarters for the (Ukrainian) SS guards
3   Administration and clinic for the SS guards
4   Tool shed for the potato commando
5   Zoo corner
6   Stables
7   Sheds
8   SS laundry
9   Planned bakery (not built)
10 Planned storehouse (not built)
11 Big depository, work site of Gold Jews

12-24 THE SO-CALLED GHETTO

12 Mess for the Jewish prisoners
13 Guards' laundry
14 Sick bay for Jewish prisoners
15 Living/sleeping quarters for the court Jews
16 Tailor shop and saddlery
17 Carpentry shop
18 Machine shop
19 Sleeping quarters for Jewish women prisoners
20 Plumbing shop
21 Storeroom for the workshops (16–18 and 20)
22 Living/sleeping quarters for Working Jews, so-called Barracks B
23 Lavatory
24 Living/sleeping quarters for Working Jews, so-called Barracks A
25 Narrow alley between barbed-wire fencing; passageway between Camp 1 (receiving camp) and Camp 2 (death camp), used only by guards and SS
26 Disrobing barracks for women, with so-called hair salon
27 Small depository at the Pipeline
28 Barracks with wood and construction materials, also the disinfectant tank
29 Motor room for new gas chambers
30 Living/sleeping quarters for Working Jews in Camp 2 (death camp)
31 Small wooden chamber with Red Cross designation, in "infirmary"
32 Refuse/garbage pit
33 Provisions storeroom for Jewish prisoners

A   Camp 1, receiving camp
B   Camp 2, death camp
C   Sorting site
D   Presorting site
E   Presorting site
F   Barracks A, clothing
G   Barracks B, miscellaneous items
H   Station grounds
I   Gas tank
J   Rail line to Treblinka Labor Camp
K   Unloading area
L   One-way track
M   Camp entrance
N   Main gate
O   Checkpoint
P   SS barracks
Q   Platform exit
R   Command office
S   Assembly (roll-call) site
T   Disrobing barracks
U   "Pipeline"
V   Fountains
W   Vegetable field
X   Lumberyard
Y   Garage
Z   Watchtower
a   Mass graves
b   New gas chambers
c   Old gas chambers
d   "Infirmary"
e   Cultivated field
f   Tank traps ("Spanish Riders"), with barbed wire
g   Incineration grate

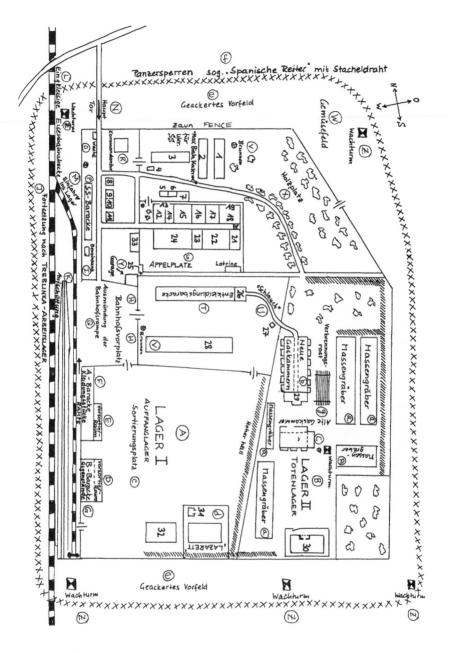

Drawn by Esther-Maria Roos, according to information provided by the author

Trap with a Green Fence

Fouling the Stars with the

Dust of the Earth

It is the beginning of the year 1940. "Non-Aryan Customers Unwelcome." The most assiduous owners had put up these signs at the entrances to their Prague coffeehouses, even before all restaurants, bars and taverns, and theaters and movie houses in occupied Czechoslovakia were required to display the official version: "No Jews Allowed."

Still, from time to time I go to the movies, not as often as I did before. I don't want anyone at home to find out.

Sometimes there is still a movie that has not yet been banned, a movie that will certainly be canceled soon and is probably now being shown for the last time. In the newsreels I see Japanese air raids on Chinese cities. Bombs fall and explode, houses crumble, fire and smoke swirl everywhere, motors and sirens scream. In the middle of some city square a young Chinese woman kneels. Her upper body rocks back and forth, her arms flailing in the air over the bloody, almost naked body of a child. Over and over again, cries and reproaches. From now on, every *mater dolorosa*, the image of every suffering mother on every altar—and there are many of these altars in baroque Prague—will remind me of this young Chinese woman.

The American film *Shangri-La: The Lost Horizon* takes place in a wonderful, lost Himalayan valley. People of many different cultures live there in eternal spring and peace. They are moderately sinful, moderately hedonistic, and they can partake of all this pleasure because, in this climate, several hundred years will pass before they become old. At night before I go to sleep I fly away to Shangri-La.

No, not to Shangri-La—in a few weeks I will be off to an isolated farm. Away from Prague, far from the gunfire—that is what my parents wanted. I am to find room and board there for as long as I possibly can. These instructions were the last words we exchanged face to face. They were to be taken away on a transport in 1941. They arranged a telephone call when they found out. To receive this call I had to go down into a small town to use the telephone in the post office. It was an hour's walk through the woods. In Prague, my parents were also calling from the post office because they were no longer allowed to have a telephone at home.

During the day, on the stony ground high over the rapids of the Moldau, two draft horses keep me company, and at night I have my books. Only in very rare instances—for example, when I have to go down into town to deliver the farmers' grain to the mill—do I pin on the Star of David. The good citizens of the town are not really all that bad, but they talk too much, and maybe they pass their stories along because they would like to see what might happen to someone who gets caught without a Star of David. Lately a lot of things have attracted attention simply because people talk too much. Silence is golden, talk is Gestapo.

Down in the town I meet a few other people wearing stars. Why do the older ones keep saying they are proud to be wearing the Star of David, that they are wearing it with a sense of honor? As I walk along beside the wagon and the horses, holding the reins in my hands, I sometimes find myself trying to hide the yellow star. On the sly I look at the people around me, searching out the ugly ones, the scarred, the cross-eyed, the lame, and the deformed ones, and I think about whom I would or would not trade places with. It's a good game. Somehow this must all have happened before, I tell myself in the evening as I lie reading in my living room–bedroom about ancient Korea, the land of so many poets, occupied and subjugated by the Japanese:

Trampled the swelling grain,
muddied the fresh dewy paths,
the stars fouled with the dust of the earth.

✿

I Know How to Handle Cattle

To another ghetto in the east" is what was written on the transport documents. The train cars were marked with the letters *Bu*. And I now had my own registration number: 639. Only four weeks had passed since I had been deported to the Theresienstadt Ghetto in the Protectorate of Bohemia and Moravia. Then I had been transport number Bg—417.

At the beginning of September 1942 they had caught up with me in my isolated little village. And now they are not even going to allow me to settle into Theresienstadt.

"A thousand head. I'm supposed to show up with a thousand head, no more, no less. And I'm warning you, if any of you dares stick his head out, it'll be all over!" The commandant, our guardian in the loud green uniform of the military police, yells so loudly that every one of the thousand people herded together on the platform at the Theresienstadt station must be able to hear him.

The train often stops, now and then for longer periods of time, especially at night. After the second night, as daylight approaches, we can tell by the signs that we must be somewhere in Poland. Shortly after midday we stop again. There is a small station house identified as "Treblinka." A part of the train is uncoupled. At the curve we can see the front cars turning onto a one-track spur. Forest is on both sides. The train travels very slowly. I can make out individual pine, birch, and fir trees.

The forest grows lighter. Everyone begins to wake up and push toward the windows, which are closed or opened only the slightest bit at the top. But no one dares look out. A high green fence, an open gate—our car passes easily through it. It is almost four o'clock in the afternoon on 10 October 1942. "Out, everyone out, hurry up! Leave the heavy luggage. It'll be delivered later!"

A platform, behind it a wooden barracks—people on the platform wear boots but are in civilian dress. That one over there has such a funny long club in his hand. It's a leather whip. They must be normal people, no Jews; none of them are wearing a Star of David. Among them stand men in SS uniforms, also with whips, and some with automatic pistols. This looks like a little train station in the Wild West, and right behind it there is a farm with a high green fence. The fence is a very pretty green. It must be a big farm with lots of cattle—and I know how to handle cattle. Everyone is being directed down off the platform through another gate and into a square. Wooden barracks are along both sides.

"Men to the right, women and children to the left! Leave the luggage. Clothes off, everything off, strip!" A few, undressed or half undressed, are shoved off to the side. They put their clothes back on. Are they going to be sent somewhere else? Somewhere better, somewhere worse? "Have your papers and watches in hand!"

In the middle, a tall SS man is explaining something with very abrupt gestures. I'm too far away to hear what he's saying. What, going to get disinfected and then sent right to work? I'm standing stark naked at the end of my row. In this weather I'm not interested in taking a bath. An SS man in a field cap hurries in from the right, down along my row, and on past me. His pace slows once he is almost past and has looked me over. Now he stops, looks back at me over his shoulder, and then turns to me: "Come on, you too—get your clothes back on. Hurry up, get over there with the others. Off with the star, no watch, no knife, there . . . you'll work over there, and if you do a good job you can get to be a foreman or a Kapo. Come on, over to your workplace, now!"

I go back out through the gate, which is covered with green branches, and then through another gate around the corner, at present half open. In passing I notice a big square, and in the square a huge pile, mountains of things—and then we're in the barracks. There is a smell of wood and mildew, and from the outside we can hear the sputtering of some machine, probably a tractor. Everywhere people in street clothes are running back and forth, carrying bundles of some sort on their backs.

"This is your foreman." A tall good-looking man in street clothes, carrying a whip in his hand and wearing a yellow armband with the word *foreman* on it, is yelling wildly at people. I don't understand what he's shouting, but I can tell from his expression and his gestures that the people running back and forth are to separate, sort, bundle, and carry off the mound of clothing that has been heaped a meter high across the entire barracks floor.

"*Du,*" I try to make myself understood in German, "what's going on here? Where are all the others, the naked people?"

"Deead, all deead—maybe not yet, but real soon, in a couple of minutes. This is a death camp. Jews are killed here, and we've been selected to help them get their work done."

Somehow he makes whatever language he is speaking sound like German. There are many words I don't understand, and I fill in with what I assume he wants to say. He is standing above me on the gigantic mountain of clothing from which the others are pulling, yanking, tugging, running in and running out. I look up at him, up there, spreading his arms wide, the whip dangling from his wrist.

"You're all from Czechoslovakia? And you don't understand Yiddish? Attention!" He nods toward the door, where a dark green SS uniform has just appeared. The arteries in his neck begin to swell, his smooth dark face turns red, his hand begins swinging the whip. "Come on, pack up those rags. Move it, damn it, move, or you won't last the day here! Hurry, hurry up and do something—like that man over there, and this one here." Out of a pile of rags I grab something that looks like a bedsheet. I spread it out, throw pieces of clothing into the middle, and start bundling the whole thing up.

"More, more, a bigger load if you want to keep your place here!" I throw the bundle over my shoulder and head for the big square outside. Just as I'm about to reach the door something like a big overstuffed bag hits me in the back. I stumble forward and just barely regain my balance. In a black uniform, a field cap on his head, very young, very healthy looking, the SS guard walks out through the door smiling, driving us on with the crack of his whip: "Ke-e-e-p moving, ke-e-e-p moving!"

Aha, you've got to run here. No walking. I can hardly get an overview of the large square. Mountains of clothing, shoes—all sorts of things are being piled up, and everywhere, a human runs back and forth in a perpetual trot, just like it was in the barracks. "Run, keep running—faster, faster." Some in black and dark green uniforms and others with yellow armbands keep yelling and cracking their whips.

Somewhere at the foot of a pile, someone takes my bundle. Running back, I can clearly make out the words on the armbands: *Vorarbeiter,* foreman, and *Kapo,* boss.

What had he said in the barracks? "Deead, all deead"—dead, everyone dead, everyone who'd undressed, everyone naked, the ones who had stayed behind the green fence. I can see the entire scene again: The train had stopped and then slowly, almost at a crawl, had turned into the forest. There was a clearing on the right that stretched over a flat plain all the way to the horizon. I could see cows grazing, being tended by a young farm boy, barefooted. It was like a scene from an old schoolbook. From a distance he stared at the train. Through the barely open window someone yelled out to him. But he was too far away to hear and wouldn't have understood Czech anyway. All he heard was a yell, and all he saw was the questioning look of the faces behind the panes of glass. He grabbed his neck with both hands, aped strangulation, rolled his wide-open eyes back, and stuck out his tongue—the way boys play their games. He stood there for a moment, and then he turned and ran back to the cows.

Now I hear the train cars rolling. The second half of the train arrives, and among the crowd I see Karl Unger with his parents and younger brother. At the end of my stay in Theresienstadt I had always stopped to talk to him when I had to pass by his bunk. He sat up top and let his legs hang down over the side, wearing short scruffy boots and looking as if he were waiting for me. Sometimes he stopped me. And I made a wager with myself, as I used to do when I had trouble in school: "If they move him out too, then we'll both be okay."

I get back to my foreman: "Hey, where do we sleep here?"

"In the barracks."

"What about food?" What kind of crazy questions am I asking anyway?

"The way things are now, you could drown in the food." He looks as if he's about to put his arms around me. Then he immediately turns cold again and cracks his whip a few times over the bundles of clothing that people are scurrying off with. "After two, three days, if you're still alive and you finally come to, then you'll know that Treblinka has everything—everything but life. My name is Leon. What's yours?"

Another group is led in. At the very moment I see Karl among them he is yelling out my name. It makes him stand out slightly from the row of people. He already knows, but there is still a question in his voice, an unwillingness to understand, as he shouts to me: "Mother, father, brother."

Toward evening whistles blow from several directions. With their whips the foremen drive us into formation, in rows five across. We march past the railway ramp down an incline to another barracks. A few pines high overhead twist, ghostlike, completely dark at the crown. Tin bowls and bread are passed out through an opening in a window. This is the mess.

I greedily slurp my ersatz coffee out of a black bowl. It rolls over the rounded edges and dribbles out the sides of my mouth, but I can't stop. I can't tear myself away from the bowl. Thirst, terrible thirst—I haven't had anything to drink for two days. Maybe that's why my head is so empty, leached so dry. No, it's been pierced by a beam, a rod, and if they pick up the rod by both ends, they can lift me up until my feet are dangling in the air; they can shove me to the ground, twist me back and forth. Someone hands me a full bowl and takes the empty one away. But he's not anyone from our transport. We are all standing here together, about twenty of us. The other man, the one who gave me the bowl, has an expression on his face that seems to say he's happy that I've come—following him, following the others.

I throw a wedge of my coarse-grained bread onto a pile of bread pieces of various sizes and origins. Dark loaves, white lumps covered with greenish specks of mold, half loaves of other breads, more and more slices stuck together in a growing pile of matter that might once have been edible.

After a short while, whistles sound again, and we're herded together, struck again and again, until we get to the barracks back up on the square where we were forced to disrobe this afternoon. Several candles flicker. Bare floor, sand everywhere. Everyone drops where he can, fighting for space, stumbles, falls over someone else. From outside the orders cut through the tumult: "Lights out, get to sleep!" A spotlight mounted on the roof of the opposite barracks is switched on and aimed at our closing doors, illuminating the entire square.

Stifling odor of bodies, wood, and the sand, which is now radiating the day's warmth. All over my body thousands of needles pierce my skin and begin to burn. The sand must be full of fleas.

We hear groans and wailing. Suddenly a moan grows into a cry and then a howl. And now it sounds as if they're fighting with someone, cursing him, pleading, comforting. That's Karl's hand I feel touching me: "It looks like someone's hanged himself . . ." After a short time everything is quiet again. And then the tone and the words slowly begin to rise above the strained breathing in the crowded room: "Jiskadal we jiskadal." Yes, I recognize it—it's the Kaddish, the Jewish prayer for the dead.

That Much Fantasy

It is difficult to say how many they chose from among the thousands who arrived on our transport—more than twenty, or fewer. A few of the faces disappeared from sight as quickly as I had become aware of them. One was said to have swallowed an entire bottle of sleeping pills. Another put an end to it all the next day in order to follow his wife and child to death.

Now I know what happened to our transport and what happens with every transport that arrives here. Before they even enter the gate, a certain number of cars are uncoupled and shunted onto the single-track siding. Sometimes there are five hundred people, sometimes many more than that, cooped up in those cars. The locomotive slowly pushes the cars through the gate. Then as everyone is getting out, the same thing that happened to me happens to them: "Everyone out, hurry up. Keep the hand luggage, leave the heavy bags here. They'll be delivered to you later!"

The masses of people are led from the arrival platform to the *Entkleidungsplatz*, the disrobing site. That is the area enclosed by the green fence where we were ordered to undress and prepare for delousing. The naked women and children were led to the *Friseurstube*, the hair salon, where their hair was cut off. The women's hair is used to insulate motors. In the meantime the men, also undressed, were ordered to stack up their hand luggage in the corner of the disrobing area nearest the sorting site. The SS men forced them into a trot. This way they drew air more deeply into their lungs, thus helping to speed things up in the gas chambers.

Together, everyone—all the shorn women and children and the panting men—is driven through the *Schlauch*, the "Pipeline," into the second section of the camp. The Pipeline is a narrow alley enclosed by barbed wire, resembling the passageway through which wild animals are released into an arena. But this alley is longer and curves in such a way that it is impossible to see one end from the other. For the most part the barbed wire is covered with green pine branches. On the dividing line between the two parts of the camp, built right inside the Pipeline, there is a small office, a depository for valuables known as the *kleine Kasse*. At the window of this small wooden shed everyone is required to hand over all papers, watches, and jewelry. Everyone is robbed of his name and another piece of his naked, anonymous life.

While the first group from the transport is circulating through the Pipeline, the cars with the next group are brought in. In the meantime, the first group has finished "showering," and before the new group enters the green passageway, the "showers" are emptied and readied for them. The transports from Darmstadt, from Theresienstadt, from anywhere in the west for that matter, whose charges are delivered in passenger cars, are handled with relative care. These passengers don't seem to sense anything amiss. All apprehension is immediately banished. No one can imagine his own end—such a very naked end.

The ones from the Warsaw Ghetto, from Grodno, and from other parts of the east are already half dead from the effects of being herded into the cattle cars, or from the journey itself. Most of these people are pushed into the middle hallway with the "shower rooms" on either side. The rest are beaten in by the SS and the Ukrainian guards. After the order is given, "Ivan, water!" a Ukrainian guard starts the motor. Instead of water the showers spray exhaust gas. It takes about twenty minutes to yield Treblinka's end product. Then slaves immediately reach for the naked, tightly packed, ashen and violet-colored results. Some pull the corpses through openings in the outer walls of the gas chambers, while specialists break gold teeth out of the mouths of the dead: "Anyone here a dentist, or dental technician, or knows something about gold—off to the side, get your clothes back on, you're going to work . . ." Others pile bodies into mass graves. Then the last steps in the process, "powdering" with lime and covering with the sandy soil of Treblinka—these are done with an earthmover, kept in continuous operation. That was the sputtering noise I had noticed on my first day in the camp.

"The sick and the handicapped off to the side! You're going to the clinic for a physical! You, old man, and you with the child, you too!"

The *Lazarett*, the "infirmary," is located at the far end of the sorting site, up against a sandy rampart, a square of about twenty-five meters on a side. Do you remember those mazes where we used to play as children? A similar entrance leads you into the camp—a narrow, crooked alley, green walls covered with a pine-needle pelt rising high above your heads. A small building with a Red Cross insignia stands at the end of the alley. There are also red crosses on the armbands of some of the people working there. Finally—here you will find comfort with these compassionate Samaritans. Not until he's inside does the limping old man from the transport catch sight of the corpses in the deep pit and the SS man with the rifle. One single *Pille,* one small-caliber bullet in the back of the neck, and every sick person, every invalid, every person handicapped in any way, anyone who might disrupt the procession to the "bath" will be liberated from his afflictions.

"Dear friend, what's wrong? Can't take this any longer? We have no use for malingerers and cripples here. Come on, come along, over here!"

"But sergeant—sir—please—I beg you . . ."

Fear and pleading work like a lit fuse: "You ass, you damned Jew swine." He has a pistol in one hand, a whip in the other, and the whip comes crashing down on the head and across the face. On reflex the victim's arms fly into the air in a gesture meant to protect his head. But the hand with the whip is ready for the next blow, a counterpunch from below aimed directly into the face.

The blow propels the bowed head back up again. The two bare hands never catch hold of the uniformed hand with the whip . . . In this rhythm the two approach the Lazarett. Now the face is nothing but a bloody distorted mask, nose smashed flat, blood streaming down from the corners of the mouth. "Undress!" They're inside, in the "infirmary." The "Samaritans" will have to tear off his clothes, stand him up at the very edge of the pit, on a slight rise, supported by a wooden pole—a springboard into eternity.

A bullet in the back of the neck, from either the pistol or the rifle, and the naked body . . . What does a naked body like this do? One may stretch itself into the air on tiptoes, vaulting like a diver from a diving board into the pit. Another may collapse immediately and slide the entire way down the sandy embankment. One may jerk its arms abruptly. Another may leap and sprawl. It's different every time. The scene is never precisely repeated. With the quiet conceit of empty mediocrity, the straw-blond SS sergeant August Willi Miete, his cap held at the small of his back, is always creating new images of the end of life and the beginning of death—this fascinating, puzzling transition.

One evening, sometime in the second half of October 1942, the sergeant on duty reports to the gaunt, ever angry SS first sergeant Fritz Küttner: "1,068 Jews dead, among them 12 women, 14 Jews infirmary."

Early the next day they will take new arrivals off the transports to replace yesterday's dead. Always there is excited anticipation among us—when they're led in, when they begin to understand, little by little. They can't fully comprehend it, they can't really believe it. No one has that much fantasy . . .

❖

The Name "Treblinka"

The name was borrowed from a small nearby village, actually nothing more than a collection of a few poor farmhouses. The nearest railway station is Malkinia, about one hundred kilometers northeast of Warsaw. The main line continues on to Białystok; leading into the camp is a single-track branch. Sand, everywhere sand, and growing out of the sand were the tall twisting pines, extruding resin, knots, and lumps. Maybe the Germans chose this sandy stretch on a bend in the Bug River, not far from the former Polish-Russian border, for the very reason that it would be easy to dig their mass graves here and fill them in again.

The entire camp covers an area of only about four hundred by six hundred meters. It is enclosed by barbed wire up to a height of two and a half meters; a dense weave of green pine branches and wire form the fence. Adding to its height, this wall of green, pine-needle pelt is built on an escarpment that is about a half meter high. On the inside, the camp is divided into various areas and yards, each enclosed in the same way, so that it is impossible to see from one part into the other. This is required by *der Betrieb,* the operation.

Everything is run by SS troops. They have young Ukrainian SS guards to help them—and us, about a thousand of us. Our number is replenished daily from the newly arrived transports. The first, larger part of the camp, the assembly area, is located between the arrival platform on one side and a sandy rampart on the other. Beyond the rampart, taking up little more than one quarter of the entire area, is the second part of the camp, the death camp. Life with its remnants still intrudes, even into the sorting site, the largest section of the assembly area; all kinds of things are there, stacked up in bizarre piles, hills, and mountains. Beyond the wall is solely the realm of death. The ones on the other side, who carry the corpses from the gas chambers to the mass graves, are closer to death than we who remain on this side. There is no return to life for anyone once the gates of Treblinka have closed behind him. There is no way back for anyone who has once stepped over the boundary into the death camp.

Most of the newly chosen workers are assigned to the commando units that work at the sorting site organizing the personal effects taken from the transports. The new ones cannot be assigned directly to the special commando units—to the "Blues," for example, the ones with the blue armbands who receive the transports as they come into the station and are responsible for moving the people and their luggage away from the arrival platform as quickly as possible, or to the "Reds," the ones with the red armbands who are assigned to the disrobing site and help people to get undressed, the ones who tear the clothes off any woman who might hesitate. This is a job for a hardened veteran.

There are poles driven into the ground at the far end of the sorting site, and on these poles are signs reading "Cotton," "Silk," "Wool," "Rags." Starting from there, and running into the middle of the sorting site, bundles wrapped in linen cloths or tied with cord are stacked up in huge piles. Items to be sorted are piled up on the near side of the site—things from the transports, things the Blues might bring from the station, things the Reds might bring from the disrobing site. Suitcases and backpacks, simple bags tied with cord that do not have handles, thousands of pairs of boots tied together and piled up into a black, scraggly, and crumbling mountain, elegant and shabby half boots, slippers, fine lingerie, tattered and infested coats.

It is all but impossible to imagine what can be found among the last things packed by thousands and thousands: a case outfitted like a small laboratory, a collapsible leather bag full of tradesman's tools, all different kinds of pass keys, an array of medical needles along with a gleaming container in which they can be sterilized. This is a huge junk store where everything can be found—except life. The wind scatters smaller items, paper money, greenish zlotys, reddish Russian rubles, German marks, American dollars, precious stones and gold, valuables that can easily be carried on your escape, a little gold heart on a chain. A black yarmulke is lying on top of a red, diarrhea-stained comforter. Next to it are artificial legs and a pair of child's crutches. Ha, ha—"Faith is my crown and my crutch"—that one's going to feed the fires in the "infirmary."

Sorting has become routine for me. I stay alert, most of all I stay alert, and that is how I work: continuously on guard, always sniffing the wind, sensing whence the next danger might come, where the warning sounds; yelled at from time to time to get working; staying alert to where the next dark green uniform with the death's-head cap might appear, alert to which direction it's going, when it turns, what might be in its field of vision, what its body language and movements might mean. Sometimes I almost feel as if I'm in training for this crucial activity, the art of survival, and that I enjoy getting better at this exciting game played for my continued existence. Anyone who works at this hectored tempo under the whip without a break, loading more and more onto his back without taking notice of when the driving rage of the SS troops and guards ebbs, will exhaust himself to the point of breakdown. Anyone who rests too long and misses the next upsurge is also finished.

When I start to get hungry I wait for the right moment, and then, with a bundle on my back, I run behind a pile of foodstuffs and jam my mouth full. Never in these past two years of war has my mouth been so full of butter, chocolate, sugar. From another pile I take a shirt, every day a clean one, every day a shirt from another dead man. Dirty clothes get unobtrusively discarded onto a pile of unsorted garments or simply tossed into the fire.

"What, paper? Just grab a piece of lingerie!" That's another way to tell who's a greenhorn here at Treblinka, someone who asks for toilet paper. We don't have as much paper here as we do silk, as long as you're not counting the banknotes. If they catch you taking anything from a pile, it's the usual punishment: first they rob you of your human face, and then there's nothing left but a naked end in the "infirmary." But it doesn't always have to be like this. It depends on which one of the SS catches you, what mood he's in, or whether by chance he's not alone. It's enough if he knows that another SS man has observed the incident from a distance. Then he'll start right in with the beating, and the second one will come to his assistance, and then it becomes a contest in which one tries to prove he's "better" than the other.

Why haven't they given us prisoners some kind of uniform? With numbers, of course. Why are we allowed to wear street clothes? We even had to remove the yellow star. It begs the question Are we still prisoners at all, Jews, or whatever else? We are no longer, we exist no longer, we're dead, in some way dead, simply because we know about it . . . Stop, you cannot, you must not think like this, otherwise you'll go off the deep end like that man last night, the one they carried off to the "infirmary" before morning roll call. Maybe the street clothes are part of the act to dupe the people arriving on the transports. This is especially true of the Blues at the arrival ramp and the Reds at the disrobing site. "*Trzymaj sie*—hold on, tough it out!" One of the people who often spoke Polish said it, and it immediately became our motto, a solution. Yes, that's it—hold on—upright—endure—assume the proper bearing! But not the way you would outside in life. Here, put on the green manchester coat with the light brown jodhpurs! Wear this, an orange silk neckerchief! Somehow this seems to impress them. They don't whip you when you're dressed like this. If your clothes get dirty or torn today, put on something more fashionable tomorrow.

Those two there in the middle, are they sorting, or are they looking for something for themselves? Hard to say. Is that one simply adjusting his boots, or is he trying on a new and better pair? Yes, pal, the more your boots shine the less you'll have to take it on the chin. Over there, there's a pile of shoe polish. If you somehow manage to use it up on your boots, you'll live to a ripe old age. Be careful not to overdo it with the smuggling and the speculation. You should look for good clothes, but not so good that they'd want them for themselves. Above all, remember: Whoever has a tired and unshaven face is flirting with the whip and the promise of the "infirmary."

What they achieve in the Treblinka death camp with a bullet in the back of the head is apparently accomplished with a hammer blow in the nearby Treblinka labor camp. The fact that the labor camp was already in existence made it easier to build the death camp. The railway branch leading to the labor camp was already there. All that was needed was a few more meters of track.

The Treblinka Labor Camp is said to have been built sometime in 1940. A sand quarry served as the foundation. Forced labor from this camp is said to have begun the construction of the Treblinka Death Camp in 1942. Good camouflage—a few people here and there knew that Treblinka was some sort of forced labor camp. The first transport is supposed to have arrived from Warsaw in July 1942. At that time only the basic facilities were finished—a few wooden barracks, a ground-level brick building with the gas chambers and the machine room, the well, the fencing. The people who were taken from the transport over the course of the day were shot in the evening after the end of the workday. The SS are said to have been even uglier than they were later, once the process became routine.

As time went by, they found carpenters and tradesmen on the transports and had them continue the construction work. They found saddlers to make whips, tailors to sew suits and uniforms, goldsmiths to sort the gold and precious stones, and even those who were to break the gold fillings out of the mouths of corpses. They found young boys to work as personal servants for the SS and a few women to do their laundry. Of those who worked in the gas chambers or at the sorting site of the operation, gradually getting up to full speed, almost no one survived for more than a few days.

Treblinka—to people outside, in life, it may sound like a friendly name.

My Next Pair of Pajamas

A row of stooped backs loaded down with bundles winds its way among the disheveled mountains of unsorted belongings and the orderly stacks of sorted "Cotton," "Wool," "Rags." Hundreds of feet tramping in unceasing double time stir up the fine sand of the sorting site. Just how had the man in front of me taken the bundle from his back and passed it off to the man standing on top of the pile? He ran his hand in and over the other man's palm. I'm curious to see if it will happen the same way the next time around. Yes, yes—he's handing over something else along with the bundle he's passing up to the top of the pile. And he's not the only one. Several others are doing the same thing. Behind me, the gaunt older man with the pale, veined face has touched me almost imperceptibly.

"You are Richard, and the one in front of you is Karl? Czechs? I am David. Stay close to me until you have sorted the next bundle. I'll tell you what's happening. We have to let the world know . . ."

And this is how David Brat, with his buck teeth and bony nose, initiated us. The two working on top of the sorted rags, stacking the bundles, are from Warsaw. They know this area and are familiar with things around here. They are going to try to escape. We are going to help them. They're going to report on what's happening here at Treblinka, to give the underground organization in Warsaw testimony about Treblinka. They, in turn, are to pass the report through the Polish underground and abroad—to England.

It was a wonderful feeling to take part, and to covertly give them money and gold I found during the sorting process. And they would need a lot of money. Much more than you could get for betraying the hiding place of a Jew.

They succeeded. The two have been gone since yesterday. Shortly before evening roll call they hid themselves among the stacks. It was all over by the time the SS counted us. Either Kapo Kurland had falsified the report from the "infirmary," stating how many of us had ended up in the "hospital" that day, and increased the number by two, or the oldest one of us, engineer Marceli Galewski, had arranged it. How did he do it? That afternoon, right under the eyes of the SS, the Blues and the Reds had smuggled two extra men out of the transports and into the work area. The total count from midday matched the evening count! But during the afternoon there had been two extra stooped backs working at the huge sorting site among the mountains of things.

This morning there are two different men stacking up bundles of rags on top of the pile. To the SS we're all alike. And if, for any reason, they should ask, the reply would be: "Sir, Herr Scharführer, sir, Sergeant Miete had him taken to the infirmary yesterday . . ."

Of course the stocky Kapo Rakowski, Moniek from the Blues, the kitchen foreman, or any of the other well-known figures could not go missing. It would have to be someone nameless and faceless from the far end of the sorting site, dusty and gray from the sand, bent over from the heavy loads.

A large convoy from within Poland delivers five thousand people in several trains. One single person is selected, one out of five thousand. In the evening, near the kitchen, when he tells us he is from Slovakia, we point out our Czech group assembled under the large twisted pine. During rest periods everyone collects around the kitchen in groups like this. They stand there with their bowls and plates in their hands, the ones from Warsaw, from Czenstochau, from Kielce, the small Czech-Moravian group, and others. Today the new one is from Preschau, in Slovakia, and his name is Zelomir Bloch. We call him Zelo. He arrived here with his wife. We don't even think of asking how he covered the great distances from eastern Slovakia, first to Dęblin, or whatever the Polish town is called, and then ended up here. He is not tall, he has more of a sturdy build, and his face, with its small mustache, is round. His thick black hair falls into waves over his high forehead. I can more easily imagine him on horseback somewhere near the Slovak-Hungarian border than in a synagogue with a prayer shawl around his shoulders. Gazing across his tin plate into empty space, he sips, he smokes, and as if from some distance away he answers our questions, which still come up from time to time.

It is always the same with the new ones at the kitchen, always the same scene, almost no outward reactions, no hand movements, no gestures. Why do I always look at the new ones this way? What am I waiting for? For him to suddenly scream, turn his hands into claws, explode, attack, tearing their flesh from their bones, roaring with rage . . . No, he won't do it. I wait and hope that he will not do it. I am relieved when I see that he is standing there, attempting nothing. Well, he's a poor shit just like me, like all of us here . . . Okay, come on, come along. You're one of us . . . If everyone is like this, if we are all like this, then maybe we're not such shits after all . . . I remember how someone passed a full bowl to me that first day, and how his expression seemed to welcome me. Tall Hans Freund turns to the new one and says knowingly, and perhaps with some relief: "Yes, my friend, they'll use you up first, before they send you to the slaughter."

Zelomir Bloch—Zelo—is still wearing his own winter coat, unbuttoned, long, reaching down over his rough boots. By tomorrow he will be wearing a *kurtka*—a short Polish jacket, a pair of elegant jodhpurs, and shiny leather boots—if he lasts until tomorrow.

A few days pass. One evening as we're being driven into the barracks to sleep, we don't immediately lie down on the sand floor. We sit together. Now for the first time, by the flickering light of a candle, we see that Zelo has brown eyes, a broad cleft chin, and a fine mouth, which somehow doesn't quite fit. Rudi Masarek is sitting next to Zelo. He has a narrow face, light skin, blond hair cut short, bright blue eyes, the chest and shoulders of a fencer. At the disrobing site his physical appearance had set him apart so dramatically that they couldn't help but pick him out. One assumes that they had never seen anyone with such perfect Aryan features, except in pictures. Rudi is a half-breed. Supposedly his mother is not a Jew. He wore the Jewish star for the first time at his wedding, and he promised his Jewish wife that he wouldn't take it off until she, a full-blooded Jew, was allowed to do the same. They arrived at Treblinka together. She was pregnant. Rudi's promise became moot here.

Hans Freund towers over all of us even when he is sitting. Words come out of his mouth in the same ambling way he moves his body. You hear in every sentence that he's a true son of Prague. Many of his expressions come from the world of commerce, from the textile business. Because of his size, Hans simply could not be overlooked upon his arrival at the disrobing site. His wife and small son, however, went into the Pipeline.

Upon the arrival of our transport, Robert Altschul had attracted notice for an entirely different reason. Almost everyone else in our transport was wearing some kind of rugged clothing—boots or high-top shoes, sports pants, jacket, cap. Robert was wearing a wide-brimmed hat, a business suit, coat, and oxfords. He had not tied his umbrella to his suitcase but was holding it in his hand. If Robert had been an old man no one would have noticed him. Old people got on the transports dressed this way. Robert made an old-young impression. This was how he appeared at the disrobing site, perhaps standing next to Karl Unger, whose body had been tanned and hardened from working at the Olmütz brick factory. Slowly and carefully Robert laid his umbrella aside, took the hat from his prematurely balding head, and rubbed his bare skin to take away the chill. A Jewish intellectual from Prague, he had spent his entire existence moving between the medical school, the coffeehouse, the German and Czech theaters, and his bachelor apartment. And now he can't even remember how it happened, whether they first noticed how careful and timid he was as he undressed for the "bath" and picked him out and then asked him his profession; or whether they first asked if anyone knew anything about medicine and pharmaceuticals, and when he indicated that he was a medic, they took him aside. We didn't have one of those yet. He would be responsible for sorting pharmaceuticals, which they had in abundance following the arrival of every wealthy transport. The residency that Robert needed to complete his medical studies would not be undertaken. His case illustrates how simply nothing more than circumstance leads to an individual's being selected from the masses.

This is how the gravediggers of Treblinka came to include such a broad spectrum of humanity: laborers, tailors, religious persons, petty thieves from the Warsaw underground, tradesmen, as well as businessmen and financiers. The so-called Gold Jews collected gold and jewelry and sorted and counted banknotes of the most varied origins, thus continuing on the inside the skilled occupations they had practiced on the outside.

Karl Unger and I are the youngest in the group. If we last a few more weeks we will celebrate our twenty-second birthdays here. The other four are in their thirties. Hans Freund looks to be the oldest.

It doesn't appear that Zelo is actually leading the conversation as we sit here on the floor using the few moments we have before we are ordered to put out the candles. One man says something, and then another, but we all look at Zelo as we speak. We will have to do something to get out of here. We find ourselves in a completely unknown land, in an alien world. The ones from Warsaw, or other places in Poland, still have some slight chance. The rest of us will simply have to endure and play for time. That means we'll have to do a damned good job of it, to get to know the SS and the guards and the leaders within our group. We will also have to become entirely familiar with the camp, all the while collecting gold and valuables. "In two, three weeks, we'll see what we can do," both Robert and Zelo are thinking.

One week or more has passed since that evening. We line up for roll call. Black boots made from highly polished fine leather, jodhpurs, belts around our short jackets, silk scarves around our necks, and the caps on our heads worn at a rakish angle—this is the way Hans Freund the clothier and Rudi Masarek the tailor had us dress. Fashionable young men from the realm of death and decay.

Everyone in camp knows the Czech group, not only our six-man team, but all twenty who had arrived on our transport from Theresienstadt and had been spared. But we are uncertain whether or not we can claim responsibility for our "success," for what has become almost three weeks of survival. Unusual changes have been taking place: people aren't being shot, rotated, or replaced as often as before.

We moved from the barracks near the disrobing site to the lower part of the camp. There is one spacious building in the shape of a large U; it is closed off at the end and contains all of our new sleeping quarters and our workplaces as well. And thus another "ghetto" has been established, one in which we are locked up at night and from which we are released in the morning. Three rooms, separated by dividers, two to the right of the entrance and one on the opposite side, are considered independent living quarters. There is even a small room between the two living areas set aside for washing up. The well is located outside the ghetto in front of the gate. It is always crowded, and sometimes there are even fights when we are herded in. Of course, most of the water for bathing goes to the successful fighters, the clever swindlers, and the ones we refer to as the "better guests."

We no longer sleep on a bare floor. There are continuous rows of bunks throughout the entire barracks, double in some places and triple in others. The six of us live and sleep together on a set of upper double bunks that abut the wooden wall separating our room from the washing area. Of course these are places for better guests, which we are, but it was Zelo who managed to arrange things. Zelo is becoming "someone" in camp, just as we all seemed to expect he would.

Our wake-up call, actually a wake-up whistle, is at six o'clock. Not long ago we had a discussion with Karl in which we all tried to figure out where our barracks elder had gotten the whistle with the shrill tone. The thing looked neither like a child's toy nor like a genuine referee's whistle. And then the tin bowls start to rattle. All we have in the morning is a black brew of ersatz coffee—no bread, no anything else. At 6:45 we go out for roll call, which takes place across the entire front of our building. The heartiness of our midday soup depends on what the most recent transports have brought in. After evening roll call we get another serving of ersatz coffee and a piece of bread. In the small bread sacks we are allowed to carry we bring better things to eat. These bags, which we carry over our shoulders, hold not only foodstuffs but also soap, shaving supplies, shoe polish, and a variety of everyday necessities, all part of a new regime. No one could say precisely when it had begun.

We were allowed to take blankets from the sorting site back to our living quarters. During the day they were to be neatly folded and stored at the head of the bunk, and everything had to be kept clean and tidy. Still, it is possible to hide all sorts of household necessities under blankets.

It is evening roll call again, leisure time in the bunks. Robert has just opened up his folding chair. He found this fisherman's chair with its linen seat up at the sorting site and risked smuggling it down after First Sergeant Küttner assigned him to work in the new sick bay. There, among the sixteen sick beds, in a small area of our living quarters, he is to continue sorting medical supplies—now in better surroundings.

"This sick bay is the best proof yet of what they are doing with us, and what they basically intend to do," Robert believes. "Every genuine factory operation needs a specialized labor force. That's why they're taking such good care of us now. And we can conclude from this that there will be many more large transports coming."

Our Rudi was recently transferred to the tailor shop. Rudi's Aryan build and athletic posture caught the attention of the fashionable and sadistic Master Sergeant Kurt Franz. He also found Rudi to be an excellent shirtmaker "from golden Prague," who sewed shirts for him and for the other SS in Treblinka.

At nine o'clock all candles must be put out, and everyone must be in his bed. I spread out my blankets and put my shoes and clothing at the head of the bed, where I can easily reach them. The silk pajamas that I have just taken out from under my bedding, and am now wearing, will be thrown away up at the sorting site tomorrow morning. After three days, actually nights, they are covered with spots of blood from all the fleas. Maybe I'll find another pair tomorrow. I'm not allowed to take things, but these days so much is being either condoned or overlooked. You just have to be careful not to fall into the hands of the meanest characters—Franz, Küttner, Miete. Maybe my next pair of pajamas hasn't arrived in Treblinka yet; maybe it's still in transit. Maybe I won't need any pajamas tomorrow. No—if I do everything correctly and well, I don't have to be afraid that some SS officer is simply going to have me for lunch.

It is becoming clear that a system of stability and specialization has been established. We processed about five thousand today. It went unnoticed that in this new, efficient organization of slave laborers, the first spark was struck that will set Treblinka ablaze.

"*Eli, Eli*—They've Thrown Us into the Fire and the Flames"

One overcast November afternoon, flames leap into the sky from behind the sandy rampart and immediately spread. We catch sight of this enormous fire-spewing stage as we are marching down to evening roll call. Our bowls in hand, we hang out around the kitchen, illuminated by the dark red glow beyond and by light from the lamps mounted on the barracks above us.

"They're starting to burn the corpses." "There's not enough room to bury them." "They want to get rid of every trace." Rumors spread with lightning speed through the camp, even before we reach our barracks. Robert is the last to crawl up into his bunk. "It's not all that easy to burn so many bodies, and especially not on an open fire like that." He continues: "Bodies don't really burn that well. They burn very poorly, in fact. You have to build big bonfires and put a lot of kindling in among the corpses, and then douse the whole thing in something very flammable. They've already had to do some trial runs."

The bread sacks lay where they'd been thrown, unopened. Everyone's eyes turned from the bunks to the few small barred windows in the barracks. Beyond the windows, red flames have spilled across the sky, coloring the entire night dark red, then orange, and finally wafting away in sulphury smoke.

Salwe appears across the way on a bunk up against the outside wall. Upright, his back to the small window, he looks into the depths of the barracks. The face, clean and bright, doesn't have a single wrinkle. The skin around his straight nose and his mouth is so fine, so vibrant. He had just begun his career as an operatic tenor when they stuck him in the Warsaw Ghetto. From there he was brought by transport to Treblinka. An acquaintance had pointed him out, and the SS selected him for their benefit, and ours. He is a small but unusually good-looking man.

No one had had to point out the fourteen-year-old Edek. With his accordion, which hid almost his entire body, he seemed—although he did not realize it—like a part of Treblinka's inventory. His parents and siblings were sent into the Pipeline immediately after their arrival. They had not played any musical instrument.

Now he's standing next to Salwe. On the bottom only his feet can be seen; on top, above the accordion, the long face with the sad eyes is devoid of any childlike features.

"*Eli, Eli*—they have thrown us into the fire, tortured us with flames. No one denied your holy writ." Salwe grieves and laments. The melody and the text from a dark past, the outside fires intruding upon the present, tear open our innermost being. We are torn apart, those of us who are hearing the song for the first time, just as those who had heard it before, in their hours of terror and pogroms, had been. "Save us, oh save us. You alone can deliver us . . ." At the end the chords disperse, and the voice breaks somewhere high over the flames: "Shema Israel . . . adonai echod!"

Hans grabs his head. "Jesus Christ, they're ready for anything. They even have a song for the fires!" The song is supposed to be more than four and a half centuries old. It is said to have originated in the days of Isabella of Castile, in the Spanish fires of the Inquisitor Torquemada, when Jews and other nonbelievers were burned under the sign of the Cross—the normal Cross, not the swastika.

Orthodox Jews do not speak the name of God. They call him All-Powerful, the Only One: *Eli, Eli—lomo asaftuni.*

I don't understand Hebrew. But I have often read the Bible, the Old Testament as well as the New. Back then, on those lonesome evenings when I fed the cows before going in. Back then, not quite three months ago. Now, here, with wide-open eyes I am listening, and the scene comes to me in which the man on the Cross screams at the ninth hour: "Eli, Eli—lama asabthani?" You, the Only One, why have you abandoned me? Yes, it must have been something like that: "and the curtain in the temple tore open . . . the earth shook . . . the peaks crumbled"—there, behind Salwe's back, behind the bars.

Jurek, the Red Kapo, is holding a bottle of vodka in his hand, bending his body forward and roaring: "Salwe—*teraz Jiddische Mamme—spiewaj Jiddische Mamme—dawaj!*" Now I know what's coming. The first time I heard Salwe sing and Edek play—not long ago, one evening in the tailor shop—the song went "*Jiddische Mamme* is the most beautiful in the world, *Jiddische Mamme, oi weh,* so bitter when she"—I don't know if the next line is "when she's not there" or "when she falls."

Salwe lives in the barracks across the way, because he's one of the "Court Jews." Today the heavens torn open in blood seem to have brought him to us. The barracks are silent until he climbs down from the bunk to leave. "We didn't have the right motivation and inspiration for this folklore. We had it too good," Robert says.

A few days after Zelo's arrival, the Sorting Commando Barracks A was set up. This was where the better items of clothing were to be sorted and processed. It is the same building where Karl and I had been brought after our arrival. This is where we had found the steaming, packed piles of textiles. But today the interior of the barracks looks completely different. The room has been separated into small compartments by dividers made of round poles; the compartments are called boxes. Hanging over each box there is a sign with instructions indicating what is to be processed and stored there. Karl and I work in a sorting operation in a back corner of the barracks near "Men's Coats Type I." Every worker in the commando unit barracks A wears a yellow armband with the letter *A*. And Zelo is the foreman. The SS noticed how the rest of us hung around him. He attracted people's attention, but he was never aggressive about it.

Facing the sorting site, a presorting shed was built onto Barracks A, thus creating a double barracks. We receive the material we process from presorting, in the same way the workers in Barracks B get their shoes, leather goods and accessories, caps, hats, and toiletries. We hear a shrill whistle from the arrival platform. The only thing separating us is a wooden wall. In the adjacent box little Abraham slides down off a stack of bundles from where he can look through a crack in the wall to the outside: "No cattle cars, they're passenger cars. They're from the west. A rich transport . . ."

Abraham has just made it back to his workplace when our new boss, Sergeant Paul Bredow, appears along with a number of other SS: "Everyone out, onto the platform!"

That is an additional job for us, the men from Barracks A. When a large transport arrives, too large for the Blues to move everyone off the ramp (that is, the platform or the train station) quickly, then we are sent in to help. The blue and yellow armbands seem to have a calming effect on the new arrivals, inspiring trust. They are a sign of order and good organization at one's destination.

From time to time, someone from the transports would ask, "Where are we, what's going to happen to us now?" and one of us would whisper, "You're heading into death—defend yourselves! It's the end for all of us!" Then they would look at us, full of skepticism and alienation, as if we were fools, assuming that in this tumult, having to worry about their wives and their children, their mothers, their suitcases and bags, they were still able to look.

From the passenger cars and a few Czech phrases here and there, I can tell that the transport that has just arrived at the platform is from Theresienstadt. The platform is inundated with luggage, and a few old people have been left behind in the confusion.

"Take that old lady to the infirmary!" The SS officer signals me with his whip.

I take the woman by the arm. Her headscarf slips down over her gray, braided hair. She looks to be in her seventies, not short, not tall. "May I ask where you're taking me?" At the end of her sentence, her helpless agitation and worry become palpable.

"To the infirmary . . ." It is not surprising, either to her or to me, that she asked in Czech and I answered in Czech. For her, this is an extension of Theresienstadt.

"And why are you taking me to the infirmary?"

"For a physical. All of the old people have to get a physical. By the way, where are you from?"

"From Beneschau. Please, may I have some water? I am awfully thirsty."

"If you can wait just a little while. Please come along, keep walking." There is a similar pair behind us, followed by an SS officer, and then others behind them. So now it's my turn. I'll have to take her all the way in, and she'll know what's going to happen . . . and she'll look at me. At the edge of the pit I'll have to tear her clothes off, maybe hold her hand, support her.

Now—I think—the decision has been made. It has fallen to you, and now the only thing you can do is what you'd imagined you'd do. The two of you will enter. You can't look at the old woman any more closely. You have to take her right up to the SS officer, apply a swift kick to his groin. You grab the pistol out of his holster, but not the Flobert he's shooting so cleanly and so silently. Of course he will keep his distance. You won't get that close to him, and the guard on top of the embankment will beat you to the draw.

We approach the green wall of the "infirmary." I let go of her arm, hoping to get away from her. But she grabs on to me, resting on the arm of my fine dark blue jacket, the one I found this morning and put on immediately. The silk invites her to hold on more tightly. "What was that? Did I hear shots?" She asks without any sign of fear, only with a somewhat agitated voice.

"No, no, it's just my friends throwing the luggage around."

I look around before entering the little alleyway to the "infirmary." The interval between the pair behind us and the SS officer has increased. The pathway is a little too narrow for two people to walk abreast. At the second curve I indicate for her to go ahead, and once she enters the curve I turn around, as if seized by some alien force, and break out, flee. At the same moment there's another shot from the inside. At the mouth of the alley I push my way past the other two. The SS man lets me go by.

I run to the barracks, but I'm immediately forced back out to the platform to finish removing the remaining luggage. On the suitcases that have come on the transport from Theresienstadt, I see the letters *Bu, Bv, By,* flying by in front of my eyes. The waste heap of belongings, of shoes, clothing, and provisions, is growing higher and higher.

You have wormed your way out. You fled—from the old woman and from the action you intended to take. So keep on enjoying what Treblinka has to offer—grub, whippings, the "infirmary" . . . What did you tell her when she asked for water? Just wait a little while, and very soon you will . . . No, I didn't tell her that. No, but you thought it. Admit it, it was something like that: In just a little while, you will have enough of everything. You damned bastard—what would you do if you had to accompany your own grandmother? Maybe she's already there, has already made her way through, already over there, and just now . . .

I am one of the last to return to the barracks. Our little curly-haired Abraham has managed to cover his face with cocoa powder from a torn box. He shakes his head and brushes away the brown powder, continuing to stuff a little more into his mouth from time to time, all the while groaning, mourning, and enthusing at the same time: "*Oy,* what a big, wealthy transport. *Oy,* what a transport!"

Death's Secret Workshop

With the tips of their shoes, the men in the first row are touching the white line drawn across the cinder-blackened assembly site. We stand in formation behind this line, with no right to life, our heads shorn and our caps in our hands. Those standing in front of us are the ones whose own lives are enhanced, the more lives they destroy.

"Stand still, do not break ranks!" Kiewe roars as he walks to the front. SS first sergeant Fritz Küttner, called Kiewe, functions as the factory manager in Treblinka. This company tyrant shows up with unexpected swiftness in the most varied of locations and succeeds in getting the entire camp to run at a feverish pace. Kiewe pulls his high-peaked military cap so far down over his face that it covers his entire forehead. It is as if his eyes are peering out of the visor into the rows and into the men standing in roll-call formation. "Camp elder, Kapos, over here, follow me!" A part of the SS unit saunters off in the same direction. Kiewe ignores the small group of women that has just approached the edge of the site, and he walks slowly through the ranks.

"You, out—no, you—yeess, step forward, you too." The whip cracks. The alarm bells stop ringing quite so loudly, because now I know what's happening. Still, I immediately steel myself for what's coming. They are looking for people for the death camp. They have to replenish the ranks of those who labor right in death's workshop. As far as I know, they never take people directly from the transports to work in the death camp. Apparently they realize that an apprenticeship in the first part of the camp is the inescapable prerequisite for work with the totally naked death beyond the fence. Those who have just come from life outside are not equipped for it.

"Well, Kapo, who are the laziest ones here? Go get them!" Kiewe acts as if the selection were being made by Kapos and foremen. They follow him reticently. The Kapo hesitates, almost imperceptibly, in front of one man; he looks another over somewhat more carefully. Kiewe whips both of them out of the ranks. They are not among the reliable. Of course Kiewe doesn't know that. The Kapos and the foremen, however, know only too well. This is how, with SS help, the slaves in this part of Treblinka silently mete out their own stern justice. It does not only happen when selections are made for the death camp. Sometimes, during the chaotic operations out on the sorting site, help doesn't arrive in time. No one can really know how much of an accident it might have been, or how much it might have been the result of one person's revenge, or the revenge of the entire group. In the meantime Kiewe has worked himself into his usual rage, has passed them all by, and is making random selections of his own from the front of the ranks. The other SS men are beating the chosen into formation at one corner of the barracks—twelve, thirteen, fourteen . . . Now, now he's coming, eyeing the man next to me. I keep my head held high by staring at the tar roof of the barracks. Gone. It's behind me, this time. Not chosen, I will keep sorting coats, shirts, shoes, keep rummaging around in piles of foodstuffs, surreptitiously stuffing my mouth full, changing into clean clothes . . .

The ones they are taking beyond the sandy embankment are descending deep into the realm of death. They will come into contact with nothing else. It is all they will have in their hands—death, but in thousands of forms composed of naked flesh. Death will stare at them out of every corner, out of thousands upon thousands of wide-open eyes and wide-open mouths. It will dangle around them with arms and legs. It will saturate them with a chokingly sweet odor. They will bring nothing from the naked bodies back with them to the barracks. They will lie down to sleep in the clothes they are now taking with them. They will eat only what the mess serves into their tin bowls. Over there a cigarette will be more valuable than dollars and diamonds are here.

The shops with tools and workbenches, the platform, the disrobing site, still suffused with the odor of naked bodies—they are all preparatory stages. At the end is the second camp, a slough with a strictly guarded secret. Even the words *death camp* are an incantation that carries the potential for danger. Among ourselves we refer to it secretively as Camp Two or "over there." Still, little by little, like water trickling through a dam, no matter how secure it was, bits of information got through to us in the first camp, and as time passed I learned more and more.

The gas chambers are the only brick buildings in the entire camp. Actually, they comprise two structures. At first was built—somewhat farther from the entrance—a smaller structure with three gas chambers, each about five by five meters. Sometime in the fall of 1942 the second building, containing ten gas chambers, was completed. This building is located very close to the Pipeline, at the point where it opens into the second part of the camp. There is a hallway running all the way down the middle of the new building. One enters the gas chambers, five on either side, from this hallway. The new gas chambers measure about seven by seven meters. The motor room is built onto the back wall, where the hallway ends. The exhaust gases from the motors are pumped into the gas chambers through conduits in the ceilings of the chambers. These conduits are disguised as showers. The floor, which is covered with coarse tiles, slopes toward the outside wall. Built into these walls are well-sealed trap doors that can be cranked open. After the "gassing process" is completed, the trap doors are raised, and the corpses are carried out onto a narrow platform. During the first phase of the operation, bodies were carried to mass graves on wooden litters that had been hastily nailed together. Now the bodies are stacked up on a large incineration grid made of train rails.

They must have started up the new gas chambers at the beginning of October, at about the same time our transport arrived in Treblinka. When all of these gas chambers are in operation it is possible to kill almost three thousand people at a time. The actual gassing only takes about twenty minutes. Much depends on how quickly the chambers can be filled and then emptied, and on how well the motors are running. The biggest bottlenecks actually occur outside Treblinka, when the railroad sidings become congested.

The most rapid work tempo is required of those who empty the chambers while the next lot is being prepared for processing in the first section of the camp. What happens to all of the straps and belts that are collected here and then brought to the entrance of the second camp? Everyone on the other side has a collection of straps. One end is looped around the feet or the arms of the corpse, and: "let's go, let's go, pull, pull!" There is no other way to get the job done quickly enough when the chamber has a full load of about three hundred.

"Right, march!" Kiewe has reached the other end of the assembly site. The group chosen for the second camp disappears around the corner of our living quarters, and we march in the opposite direction back up to work.

"Sing a song!" The order to sing is passed on from the dark green and gray-green SS officers, through the Ukrainian guards, to us, and we hear: "Seeeng soonng, *job twoju matj*, fuck your mother. Sing, you sons of bitches!" From Ukrainian the caterwauling turns into Polish. Back and forth alongside their units, the Kapos and the foremen in yellow armbands leap and howl.

"Hey, you, march, one-two, one-two, can't do it, can't get it?" No one would imagine that this shrill metallic voice belongs to such a small body, that this Berlin dialect is not coming from an SS officer but from one of our three bosses. They are German Jews to the SS, and Jewish Germans to those here who are the most wretched. This man is Kapo Mannes, straightforward in his movements, precise in his actions, his brown face clean. In the last row of his unit there is a little man limping along, a man without a name, without an age, from somewhere in the Jewish quarter of a village near Warsaw. Kapo Mannes doesn't want members of his unit to feel the whip. Little Kapo Mannes with a big voice, walking tall, wants his unit to march faultlessly, wants everything to be orderly. Kapo Mannes shows the little man, encourages him, warns him of approaching danger, raises his voice almost to a roar, and then lowers it to coerce. Even if Kapo Mannes is not the one threatening him with a whip, the little man raises his arms in defense, moving his entire body as if to avoid a blow, answering everything with his whining questions: "*Oy*, Kapo Mannes, what for do I have to march in Treblinka, what for do I have to sing?"

For Adrian, who is by far not so shy, marching in step is simply alien, not kosher: "*Oy*, Kapo Mannes, what kind of a Jew are you? A German Jew? A Yiddish German? You know, to me you're just a piece a shit!"

※

Ten for One

This time the sound of the arriving cars is somehow different. After the squeal of the brakes and the cough of the locomotives stops, whistles blow. We are chased out of the sorting barracks. Freight cars are parked along the platform. Along with the Blues, we open the cars. From the inside there is no pressure on the sliding doors. They're easy to open. The cars are empty.

Staff Sergeant Stadie is standing near the entrance to the camp with some kind of weapon slung over his shoulder. More people from the sorting site are being herded over to the platform, SS officers whipping and kicking some of them until they fall to the ground. The guards, ambitious apprentices that they are, follow suit. Even their commander is present, Chief of Guards Rogoza, a boyish, red-cheeked boor.

Now we begin to understand the commotion! They have a new project; they are directing a new scene, which they haven't yet rehearsed and practiced. Everywhere around us we hear the cracks of whips and shouting, until we're standing in a long row: "On the double—load these cars!"

A huge line begins moving back and forth between the pyramids of sorted bundles at the sorting site and the cars at the platform. Before I come running up to the platform with my next bundle, the first car is full, and the second almost full, then a third and a fourth . . . Most of the foremen are waving their whips through the air and accompanying this directorial gesture with rhythmic shouts.

All of the cars at the platform are fully loaded. The SS troops go from one to the other, checking them and ordering the sliding doors to be closed. The train leaves, and after a short time the locomotive pushes more empty cars up to the platform. "Well, that's a crazy transport," says Hans Freund, towering over the entire row, overlooking everything. "The things that are left are all practical things, useful here and at the front."

Those days at the end of November, the beginning of December, the number of arriving transports decreased, but the activity in the first camp was still intense. Cars bringing humans to Treblinka alternate with cars taking things away from Treblinka. With few exceptions, the cars used to bring people to the camp were not used to haul sorted cargo out. The covered cattle cars carrying people came mostly from Polish villages, the empty freight cars mostly from Germany. The mountains of bundled things on the sorting site, as well as the piles inside the barracks, disappeared, and new ones grew to take their place, like a scene from a trick film. If I were an SS officer I would know that even this "human pack" is capable of organizing itself, after it has been running in line, back and forth for two, three days, and all it's doing is loading freight cars. One of them will know who's running in front of him, and who's in back, who's taking on the bundles, who's stacking them up in the cars.

I would have seen through what recently took place. All of a sudden three or four bodies carrying bundles collide at the door to the freight car, and they all fall down. Two foremen immediately start whipping them. Even the camp elder, Galewski, jumps into the fray, shouting. Then a foreman beats someone away from one of the cars, and Sergeant Gentz could not keep from turning around and observing "how these Polish shits are going after each other." By that time the two in the car were already covered with bundles, hidden. The car was ready to go. "Close the doors, sir?" If I were an SS officer I would have heard more in this inane question. The fully loaded train leaves, and on board are two more who "must let the world know." This is all accompanied by a skillfully staged commotion. And the main characters—apart from the two escapees—are the ones who are always getting pushy at the mess, the ones who are filching things right from under your nose. If I were an SS officer . . . these words and these thoughts keep coming back to me.

Shortly after that, two events take place that stifle any sense of satisfaction and break the will to escape from Treblinka. Shortly before the departure of one of the freights, the inquiring sergeant first class, Boelitz, always more staunch and more thorough than the others, discovers two men from the sorting site hidden in the undercarriage of one of the cars. Lalka appears immediately, because this is now his responsibility. He doesn't walk; he strides. He is aware of every one of his steps. He knows that everything about him is flawless, perfectly pressed, polished bright: the black boots, the gray jodhpurs with the large yellow leather patches stretching across his rear and down to his knees, the green uniform jacket, the gray deerskin gloves, the skull and crossbones cap worn at an angle. SS master sergeant Kurt Franz knows only too well that here he is the most highly cultivated, the most handsome of all. What he doesn't know is that among the damned here in Treblinka his appearance, his red cheeks, his sparkling brown eyes, have earned him the Polish nickname Lalka—the Doll.

The other SS officers are just standing around, as if waiting for a show to begin, a show featuring humans who have come to look much like naked scarecrows. The two will be forced to undress on the platform. The guards come running, on orders, expecting some novel form of "amusement." They drag the two men by a rope tied around their necks, beating their naked bodies all the way down to the mess. There the men are hung by their feet, heads down, from a beam fastened between two trees.

"Look at those two very closely!" The hand in the gray deerskin glove is pointing from the roll-call site around the corner of the barracks in the direction of the mess. "Learn this lesson, you dreamers, you monkeys—should another of you contemplate anything like this! Dismissed!"

The commotion around the mess continues to grow. The amount of food being brought in by the dwindling number of transports has shrunk. An image turned on its head, as if in a funhouse mirror, intrudes into the steam rising from the bowls in the raw cold and the stale odors of the kitchen: bluish bodies, heads forced back, protruding Adam's apples, eyes seeming to spill out over their foreheads, thick ribbons of blood between the nose and the lips, thin ribbons of blood from the corners of the mouth to the temples.

"*Shema Israel*—hear me, Israel . . ." Out of the death rattle comes what is both a prayer and a call to battle. Then a quiver goes through one body, as if it had wanted to catch itself with the hands tied behind its back, and then these words burst forth from the bleeding mouth: "What do you think you're doing! Spit that garbage out! Take revenge!"

And the same scene plays out again, when two more men are

dragged out of a loaded car. It is not entirely clear if they were about to hide themselves or if they had somehow gotten buried under bundles they were stacking inside the car. This time—it was shortly before noon—the guards called the carpenters, and shortly after that there were two large wooden poles rising out of the ground in the area of the train station. Crossing between the two poles was a third, and the would-be escapees were hung from it as a warning to us. When we marched back from our noon meal they were already silent, and an idiotic observation occurred to me: "So, that's what a naked man looks like upside down." After a while they were cut down and carried off to the "infirmary," and the gallows were also dismantled.

A few days later Zelo conducts our evening bunk meeting more quietly than usual, but all the more intently, in a way only he can do: "It's about time we did something. Winter's on its way, frost and snow and then . . ."

"Well then, our feet might freeze off if they hang us up naked," Hans Freund chimes in.

"I talked to a man today. His name is Kohlenbrenner. He claims to have a plan that would get all six of us, and him, out of here. At night, past the guards, it's not so bad. Our barracks isn't locked. And since I'm a foreman, I could call the Ukrainian guard on duty over to the door. We could get him involved in a little commerce. We could make a deal with the guard who has night duty, and tell him we'd set out some money in a pouch at the door, and he'll get us some vodka . . . this kind of thing's been going on here for some time. The transports aren't the only source of vodka for the Blues and the Reds. Some of you will stand behind the door, and when he gets close enough we'll jump him as quietly as we can. One of us puts on his uniform, takes his gun, calls the SS man on night watch at the ghetto gate, and we'll have to take care of him too. His coat, his cap, and his automatic pistol should help us get past the guard at the front gate and on out over the tracks. That is the shortest way. If we can get ourselves out this way and take Kohlenbrenner with us, he has promised me he will take us to Warsaw and get counterfeit papers for all of us."

"That means we'll have to be taking lots of money and gold with us," Robert adds.

"And just how did this guy come our way?" Hans jumps in again.

"He's got other buddies here, and he doesn't really know us well enough."

"And we don't know him either," Robert says, "but, for the six of us, it is our only option."

"He's not interested in trying an escape with the people he knows. He knows too many people," Zelo explains.

"He knows them all too well," Hans observes.

"With forged papers we could join the underground in Poland, work with the partisans, or volunteer for work in Germany."

"And why did he make his way to Treblinka, when he could have gotten all that done for himself a long time ago in Warsaw?"

"Because he didn't believe it either. He heard rumors here and there, but he just couldn't believe it. He trusts us."

"Trusts—trusts, because of that Aryan mug on Rudi and Karl that'll make his escape a lot easier."

Hans is gesturing with his shaving brush. "And he's counting on us to be ready for a fight if it comes to that. He knows we won't shit in our pants like his dear friends. Rudi made it to lieutenant in the army, and so did Zelo, but this shithead from Warsaw wants to give us hints about escaping, and we'll be the bodyguards."

"*No, czloveku, na Treblinku to nie je taka zla ponuka*—hey, for Treblinka, that's not such a bad deal." Zelo mixes Slovakian, Czech, and Polish expressions together.

"And what's going to keep him from abandoning us somewhere on the outside? Somewhere in Poland?" Hans worries.

"May I be abandoned on the outside by someone, somewhere, anywhere in Poland!" Karl pleads.

The conversation loses focus: "If we get caught here on the inside, we'll be hung by our feet, naked. That won't take too long—about twenty minutes and you're unconscious. Twenty minutes isn't long enough for you? We can't let it come to that, we have to jump them immediately and finish them off on the spot—and if the German military police or the secret police, or whatever they're called, catch us, have you heard what happens if they catch you without papers? They strip you naked and take a good look at your identification: no foreskin. And then they go a few rounds with you before you can get cold. Rudi has the best build for an SS uniform, but once we're on the outside it'll be better to get rid of it."

"In a week, at the latest, we should give it a try." Zelo is speaking coherently again. "Rudi and I will try to find out if there is a change of guard at night, and how it works. The rest of you get all of the money down here from the coat boxes. When we go, everyone should be carrying some kind of provisions, a knife, and some rope or leather straps."

Two days later the barracks guards do not have to wake us. Every one is up long before the whistle blows. Restrained, excited voices fill the barracks. Seven of the Blues tried to make a run for it, in a way similar to what we have in mind. But the guard at the ghetto gate was quicker. He called in the SS on duty, and reinforcements too. The numbers of all seven were taken down, and then they were driven back into the barracks and put under guard. All of that took place in the quiet between two and three o'clock in the morning. This was the first time that the numbered cloth triangles had proved themselves to be of use; we had each gotten one of these little triangles at the time we moved into the ghetto. They were to be worn on an outer layer of clothing on the left side of the chest. "They let themselves be driven back in." Robert spoke more deliberately than usual. "And I always thought the Blues knew what was up."

At roll call there is an unusually large number of SS troops. There must be around twenty. Franz, "the Doll," steps up and begins his presentation: "Today is the last time we will mete out mild punishment." In a relaxed stance and tone of voice, he continues: "The seven of you who tried to escape will be shot." Suddenly he raises his voice: "From today on, I am making every Kapo and every foreman directly liable, with their own lives, for their people. For every one person who escapes, or tries to escape, ten men will be shot—for one, ten others! Now, every Kapo and every foreman will be present at the execution in the infirmary! Dismissed!"

We march off and spread out through the work barracks on the upper level. "But they weren't tortured," someone observes. Then in the ensuing silence following the seven individual shots, he repeats pensively: "For one—ten."

✿

The Hangmen and the Gravediggers

One could use the terms *masters* and *slaves* for every being who walks on two legs here in Treblinka. But such appellations are only useful as titles. Otherwise, things in Treblinka are not all that simple. There are greater and lesser masters. There are half masters, commanders of hangmen, master hangmen and their assistants, and more or less living slaves. Gravediggers, greater and lesser.

Everyone keeps watch and observes the others and his own. Everyone behaves differently when he's in a group, and differently when he's alone and no one of higher rank is looking on. Everyone has been besotted by growing piles of belongings and valuables left behind by hundreds of thousands of people. Everyone plunders and speculates. The masters of the SS and the guards are most interested in gold, jewelry, money, fur coats, in any event, no matter whether the war is a success or a failure. Slaves grab for food and valuables too, just in case that one and only chance might arise.

Everyone is curious and anxious to know what the next transport will bring to Treblinka. Even the ones at the far end of the camp, in the death camp, can judge the status of a transport by the gold that is broken out of the teeth, or perhaps by the examinations that are made from time to time to see if the corpses might have gold or jewelry in any body cavities other than their mouths.

Everyone sings and lets himself be serenaded: the Germans "*Heimat* . . . your stars," the Ukrainians "*Oj pri luczku, pri szirokym poli* . . . in the meadow, in the broad, open fields," the Jews "*Stejterle Bels*, my beloved Bels . . ." and "*Jiddische Mamme*" and "*Eli, Eli* . . ."

On top of the sandy rampart a distant figure promenaded and then stopped from time to time. It was a few days after they had started burning the corpses. From there he viewed his estate. He looked down to one side, where he could see the smoke rising into

45

the air and forming a majestic stage set. Then he looked to the other side, where below him the mountains of things and chains of tiny figures continually changed shape and, like a kaleidoscope, presented ever-evolving images. He didn't carry a heavy bullwhip like all the other SS, but only a light riding crop, and he always wore light-colored deerskin gloves and a field cap on his head. A few fingers of his right hand hooked into the front of his fitted green uniform jacket. He is the camp commandant, SS captain Franz Paul Stangl. Just as he looks down from the berm, standing up there by himself, alone, he keeps his distance from everyone and his perspective over everything from above. He rarely comes up to the operation from his headquarters in the lower part of the camp, avoiding all contact with the Jewish workers and Ukrainian guards. When he does appear at roll call, he does so only to look in on events from the sidelines, from the corner of the barracks. And then, tapping his riding crop lightly against his boots, he leaves before the end of roll call, without saying a word. With his slightly bent nose and prominent chin, by the relaxed bearing and movements that are a sign of the upper ranks, he gives the impression of being the lord of the manor, meting out power among the other lesser lords. Robert says that this exalted lord knows more than the others and will also have more on his conscience. He is in a position where he needs neither to fire a shot himself nor to wield a bullwhip.

Almost everyone is given a nickname. Pseudonyms are used for all sorts of things, because we need communications and warning signals that we understand—and no one else. Among these are three special signals for deadly danger, which also refer to the main pillars of Treblinka and its operations. We only know their real names from what we have heard. We don't know how they are spelled: Franz, Küttner, Miete.

The first time I saw Franz in action was on the second or third day after my arrival. I came out of the barracks and went up to the sorting site, and I saw, only a few meters away, how he had got one of the slave laborers where he wanted him and had begun to apply a good twenty-five to his backside. Every blow was delivered with a full stretch, stroke, and follow through, as I know it from tennis, with style. But this was only a sideshow. It is the grand performances, staged for everyone at roll call, that bring his smooth cheeks to their full redness. Franz "Lalka" (the Doll) is more or less the second in command in this operation and was probably put here to keep an eye on Stangl; in turn, the experienced martinet Küttner was probably brought in to keep an eye on Franz. Lalka is here for looks, for extraordinary and grand events. Küttner-Kiewe manages everyday operations, takes care of the routine. His eyes see into every corner; he rushes past the workshops, beats someone bloody because someone is too slow; and then in an instant he's up in Barracks A cracking his whip above our heads. His favorite move is a blow to the face with a loud, full crack. All of his movements—and even his language—are abrupt. Everything is "slam-bam," in contrast to Lalka's basically athletic appearance. In civilian life Franz was a cook, most likely a very stylish chef. Küttner brings a lot of history with him to Treblinka: he is said to have been a chief of police and jail warden.

Silently, like a ghost, Sergeant August Willi Miete shows up everywhere where someone is giving out, where someone has been marked and branded, where someone can no longer pretend that he is healthy and working at full strength. His nose and his entire face are somewhat bent to the side. His long legs attached to a short torso carry him along in a rocking motion. His cap—the SS field cap— sits on his head pushed back over his straight blond hair. And his fish eyes, as if they meant to give comfort, say: "Now, come, come along. Now you will be able to rest. But you'll have to prance in front of me like a little lamb. Otherwise I'll start shrieking in my falsetto voice and prove to you that I'm better at it than the elegant Franz or the martinet Küttner." One nickname is not enough for him. The Murderous Pussy-Footer, the Meticulous Janitor of Treblinka, has several others: in Czech he is the Good Hunter, in Yiddish Crooked Mug, and, the most fitting, the biblical Malchamoves, the Angel of Death, for his is the realm of the "infirmary." Somehow always unkempt and disheveled, Willi Mentz, with a black mustache under his nose, is subordinate to Miete in civilian as well as in military life, although he too is a sergeant. In real life he is a dairy farmer, and here he is marksman second class. He is responsible for the routine shootings that take place in the "infirmary" as the transports arrive. He shoots and shoots, and keeps shooting, sometimes moving on to the next target even when the previous shot had not found its mark and a sentient victim simply slipped into the fires. Messy work.

We found out that there were always groups of SS going on leave at six- to eight-week intervals. Rudi, down in the tailor shop, is the first to notice when they are getting ready to go. Next, we see it in the foot traffic up here in the clothing barracks.

Sergeant Paul Bredow, head of Barracks A, comes all the way back to our corner, to the box "Men's Coats Type I." He moves with a gliding step, as if he were on a parquet floor, as if he were still wearing the waiter's jacket that he wears in civilian life. And he's bringing a rare guest with him, Sergeant First Class Pötzinger from Camp 2.

"Let's see, have you got anything here?" Bredow starts in. He's been doing this every day for a week now. He wants to have a splendid, flawless coat. He examines every coat carefully, checking to see that the collar's not worn, or the pockets torn. He also looks at the lining. He's interested in something plaid, and a belt would be fine. He's got a minor problem, though: he keeps looking around for a place to set his whip down, until Pötzinger, who's been watching the entire process, ends up holding it for him. When he tries a coat on, Bredow always turns up the collar until the tips touch his long sideburns. The sideburns and the long curling mustache are no doubt an attempt to compensate for what he lacks upstairs over his fleshy pale face.

Pötzinger starts trying things on, rather hesitantly, as he is well aware that it will be difficult to find something to fit his large stocky figure. When he gets close and lowers his head, his curly hair struggling out from under his military cap, he exudes the sickly sweet smell of the second camp. His boots are dirty, and even his uniform is somewhat wrinkled. Over there, where he comes from, all of the work is fieldwork. Not even the SS over there can comport themselves as elegantly as the ones over here.

In the end, they're both interested in the same coat. They start trying to convince each other that the coat really doesn't fit the other —for that one it's too large, for this one it's too small. Sergeant Bredow, as head of the clothing barracks, gently pulls rank on Sergeant First Class Pötzinger. The scene is broken up by the appearance of the high-peaked cap of Küttner-Kiewe. Bredow orders me to take the coat down to the tailor's shop after lunch so it can be pressed, and later he'll pick it up himself. Both of them turn and walk away toward Küttner. Matthes, head of operations in Camp 2, as Küttner is here, has to take better care of his reputation. Supposedly he is also one of the main pillars of Treblinka.

"Remove every Star of David. No one is to know it has ever been there . . ." David Brat, from the box across the way, is standing behind a table under the sign "Men's Coats Type II," and training a new arrival. The top of David's head just reaches the trainee's chest, and David almost shrinks into obscurity. This steamroller, with little eyes and a long curling mustache under his nose, is called Willinger. The foremen outside at the sorting site managed to get him in here after playing a little scene for their SS masters. These are the opening moments of a grander play that is now in preparation. "Empty all of the pockets, look through them, check the entire coat manually to see if there is any money, gold, or valuables sewn into it. And see that little box hanging over there? You throw everything into that box." David hesitates briefly and then continues very deliberately, saying something in Yiddish that sounds like *as oser* (use your head), while making the gesture for a "long nose."

"Well," David stops again and changes his tone, "we have to throw something into the box. We can't send those guys back down to the ghetto empty-handed." With a nod of the head he points out two men who happen to be walking slowly through the barracks. On their upper arms they are wearing yellow armbands with the inscription "Gold Jews," and they are carrying small chests in their hands. Several times a day these gold and jewelry sorters make their rounds through the camp, going through all of the work barracks, emptying all of the boxes, collecting the valuables that have been found, and then returning to their worktables in the big depository, where they sort and pack everything. Even though the chests of the head gold sorter no longer are filled nearly so full as they were when one transport after the other was pulling into Treblinka and we were not yet as practiced as we are now, the Gold Jews still make their regular rounds, as they have been ordered to do. In this way we have been able to open up lines of communication between the lower and upper parts of the camp. There is contact between the ghetto and the workshops even during working hours.

"This is how each coat is folded and tied, ten to a bundle, and the bundles are then stacked up here in the box." David has ended his lesson. Then I hear the words *spot check*. David is warning the trainee that the SS especially like to make very thorough spot checks here in Barracks A, threatening a trip to the "infirmary" if things aren't perfectly sorted and packed.

Warning signals reach us from the depths of the barracks. Sergeant Hirtreiter is on his way. Among ourselves we refer to him as Sepp, the same thing his SS buddies call him. Coarseness characterizes his dark face, with its protruding cheekbones and thick lips, just as it does every one of his movements and his speech. He looks a few coats over very quickly, rolls one up under his arm, and strides off with a long and easy gait, absently mumbling from habit: "Let's go, let's go, quick, quick . . ."

"He's really hard on women," Hans Freund says.

The next customer is Sergeant Karl Schiffner, whose face looks as if it's been lightly powdered. He displays a row of gold teeth when he speaks: "Now, I'd like to see if I can pick up something decent here." He throws a pack of cigarettes onto the sorting table. Even three weeks ago they wouldn't have been worth much. But now that there aren't so many transports, they are beginning to take on some value. With an easy gesture Schiffner adjusts his cap. His fingernails are manicured, his black hair combed smooth and parted in the middle. He leaves, the coat folded and carried over his arm. Supposedly he is a fellow countryman from Töplitz-Schönau, a German-speaking territory of the former Czechoslovakia.

Good citizen, a civilian in uniform, and supposedly the oldest among the SS here, Sergeant Karl Seidel comes in. He always addresses us impersonally: "Away with that, this comes over here, that goes over there . . ." But this time he turns and speaks directly to me in a quiet voice: "If you can come up with a decent winter coat . . ."

Politely, right to me, "you," but he didn't say please. Or did he? Damn it all, why don't I just kick him in the balls, why don't I tighten this belt around his neck until his eyes pop out, just like the two guys who were hauled off to the mess to be hung upside down by their feet? And what would you achieve by doing that? Whom would you be helping? Everyone else would just watch without moving a muscle. You'd have to finish yourself off too, if you didn't want them to get you . . . So, so fantasize a little more while talking yourself out of it, dig around in this pile and look. "Dark blue, if possible, or dark gray . . ." for the graying Mr. Seidel with his straightforward face and polite demeanor.

Sergeant Gentz and Sergeant First Class Boelitz appear in the walkway among the boxes deep in the barracks. "Aha, they'll be my customers," we can hear Hans Freund say from the adjacent box, under the sign "Women's Coats Type I." He's wearing a long white coat that reaches down to the ankles of his highly polished boots and makes him look even taller than he is. He has a wide belt around his waist and a Russian fur hat on his head. The fingertips of his wool gloves have been cut off so that he can sort more efficiently. He wears this white smock when he works in the box. Supposedly lice are less attracted to white.

"Look, now they're at 'Bras and Panties.'" Without looking at it, Hans feels through the coat he has in process on his worktable. With his eyes, with his voice, actually with his entire body, he is following the figures in uniform. From his table he can't see what's written on the signs above the individual boxes, but he proves to us and to himself how familiar he is with this entire setup: "Oh, yes, it's probably best to start at the far end, at 'Bras and Panties.' Stockings are only available in packages of fifty, gentlemen, corsets in packages of twenty-five, and as you see, here we have men's shirts, twenty-five to a package, slacks ditto, children's underwear—not interested? The two of them usually come over here to me. Gentz has been after me for several days to find him a Persian lamb. I've slashed quite a few, but for him I'll have to come up with something good. They should get to know me. Today they'll get everything free. Persian lamb, beaver, muskrat, everything for their dear SS ladies at home, and for their hookers too. Who in Greater Germany these days can compete with Hans Freund and Company, Women's Coats, Treblinka?"

Boelitz certainly didn't come here at his own initiative. Gentz will have led him astray. If I imagine Gentz without the SS uniform, he could be a nice, bright young man. I imagine him tossing his school bag into some corner and putting the field cap on his straight, bright red hair, buttoning his uniform jacket, grinning at the reflection in the mirror of the youthful freckled face with the strawberry blond eyebrows, and thinking: "This is gonna be fun." And when he got to Treblinka, and everyone around him eyed him with awe, then he told himself: "Well, whadda ya know, this is fun."

Boelitz is quite another type, made of more solid stuff. He is a strong, lean young man. It's not just that his hair is cut short, shaved high in the back, but it's also the impression that the sun has bleached the eyebrows and lashes blond on his oval, rosy pink face. He doesn't bellow and get excited like Küttner and Franz, but the blows he administers with care and some zeal are just as terrible. His comrades may well say that he eats and drinks duty and that he's ambitious. He would like to be able to do a lot of the things they do, but he can't. At most he might watch while his buddies—assuming Küttner and Franz are nowhere in sight—pick pretty and valuable things out of the piles. He can't forbid them to do it. He's one of them. He can't blow the whistle on them. He just wouldn't be able to.

This man is lonesome at Treblinka. Now he's standing in front of the box "Women's Coats Type I," watching, a little embarrassed, a little disdainful, and a little curious, while Gentz has Hans show him a number of coats. And Gentz, it seems, is playing a little game with Boelitz: "Step up a little closer," Gentz says, holding a Persian lamb coat in his direction. The whip in his other hand looks as if it's something he'll use to beat the coat. "Well, what do you think?"

"Nothing, a piece of shit." At the moment Boelitz can't express himself any other way.

"Not a piece of shit. This is a genuine, fat-assed Persian lamb. Isn't that right, Hans?" Gentz already knows Hans by name.

"Yes, sir, sahhgent, faddass perzhun." Hans lets his home dialect show. With his light red hair and his freckles he looks like a young brat.

"How much can a piece a shit like that be worth, anyway?" Boelitz asks.

"Ohh . . ." Hans, his hands gesturing happily, begins to explain furriers, pelts, sheep, auctions. The barracks with its boxes has become a large sales hall full of clothing and furs, and the expert Hans Freund elucidates, compares, offers, sells.

"Come on, get something yourself," Gentz exhorts Boelitz again.

And Hans understands what's happening, joins in the game, and exclaims officiously: "Well, well, sahhgent!"

Master Sergeant Lindenmüller, somewhat older, much more mature than Boelitz and only superficially a similar type, comes to Barracks A before Christmas with something other than shopping on his mind. He stops in the office, which is right at the main entrance, and once he is alone with Zelo he begins speaking to him as if making a report: "Come from a military family, am a convinced

National Socialist, but I cannot reconcile what is happening here with my sense of military honor, will go on Christmas leave beginning tomorrow and will never come back here, have volunteered for the front, would like one of you to know, and I chose you . . ."

The Ukrainian guards—they are the slave drivers and hangmen's helpers; they are despised by the masters and the master hangmen and by the slaves, the damned, as well. Every one of them is young, somewhere around twenty, and they are all bursting with health and vulgarity. They could not have dreamed—when they came out of the villages and hamlets and let themselves be recruited—that they would be swimming in grub, vodka, and money, that the women, the girls, would follow them into the villages around the camp, about to hike up their skirts. It seems to them that they could keep right on beating and killing Jews just as they were used to doing back home. But here is where they will really get down to business. It took the *Germancy* to really get things going. Rogoza, the head guard, is the only one with a last name. Everyone else is Sashka, Grishka, Ivan. The SS officers address them "Hey, guard, we're talking to you, *panye*—Mr. Guard," and communicate in a mixture of Slavic languages. From the remoteness and the utterly endless distances of their homeland they have brought a rare gift with them: spectacular song. In the heavy twilight and the early morning hours, at the changing of the guard, one single column sends a plaintively wild song soaring into the air high above the tightly packed crowns of the pines, finally wrapping all of Treblinka in a multipart chorale.

As our supplies of food begin to fall off, and then the clothing and valuables, as the extravagant bounty of Treblinka is dispersed, disappearing in all directions, and is not replenished by more transports, these robust, greedy boys stride past us in their black and brown uniforms, repeating over and over again: "*Davaj hrosche*— give us groschen, and there'll be bread, and ham, and vodka." They never forget to keep an eye out for the worst of them—Franz, Küttner—and the worse ones, too—Miete, Boelitz.

The gravediggers, the real ones and the most wretched, are "over there" beyond the berm. But not all of them lay their hands on naked death. The camp elder—supposedly his name is Singer and he comes from Vienna—the Kapos, and the foremen all work with whips in their hands, the barracks people with brooms. The ones who move the corpses around from one place to another on their slipshod wooden litters don't have to come into direct contact with naked dead bodies, the way the ones do who load and unload the corpses. The one who washes off the gold somewhere in a little shed only sees teeth and pieces of gum. He holds nothing but small bits of death between his fingers. Some of the very few women suffer the same fate as most of the women here in the first camp: all of the dirty wash gets thrown at them.

Even here in the first camp there are three genuine and miserable gravediggers. These three "Samaritans" with Red Cross armbands are responsible for burning bodies from the "infirmary" on a heap in the pit. Then there are the nameless "shit sweepers" here at the sorting site, only sometimes haulers of dead bodies, the half dead, and the immobile taken off the arriving train cars.

At a much higher rank are the "experts" in the clothing sections of Barracks A and the accessories sections of Barracks B. They have a roof over their heads during most of their working hours. In the barracks, which are lit only through a rather long and narrow skylight and a window in each end wall, they are less exposed to fields of sight and to the shooting range. They have more of an opportunity to conserve their physical strength.

The Blues at the arrival ramp, and the Reds at the disrobing site, still work with the living. They have gradually turned themselves into a group of thick-skinned toughs. The only dropouts were the ones who couldn't take the undressing, especially the women undressing. The other slaves, and even the masters, each in his own way, show a certain grudging respect for them and the way they do their sensitive jobs: the SS troops because everything works, and us—well, as long as none of them fall on their faces, none of us will become replacements.

Once—it can't have been very long before we got to Treblinka—there was someone who gathered everything he still had in him and jumped one of the death's heads with a knife. This is how the living quarters of the Ukrainian guards got renamed the Max Biala Barracks, in memory of the stabbed SS man. He is supposed to have been even worse than Küttner-Kiewe and Franz-Lalka. The man who stabbed him was named Berliner, or something like that. He was probably that strong and courageous because he had just returned to Poland, his home country, after having spent several years abroad. And he found a good end after his deed here at Treblinka: they beat him to death on the spot.

Since the number of transports has decreased, the Blues and the Reds have become all-purpose commandos. Together they take care of the train station, sometimes they're set to work at the sorting site, and of course they help load cars with bundles of sorted items. It seems to me that the SS have them on a longer leash when they're not engaged in their main line of work, for which they have been specially trained.

The term *Court Jew* no longer has the same meaning it once had. Back then, at the time of the greatest chaos, before things stabilized, slaves were destroyed from one day to the next, from one hour to the next, and new ones appeared. Miete himself must have had at least eight a day on his conscience. But it gradually became clear that measures would have to be taken to safeguard the tradesmen and professionals who had been selected for furniture making, carpentry, mechanical work, and construction, for sorting gold, money, and jewelry. This also included numerous women and children who had been assigned cleaning and laundry duties. They had to be marked in some way to keep them from being immediately slaughtered. And this is how the yellow armband with the inscription "Court Jew" came into being. After a certain period of time one got to know their faces, simply because the Court Jews stayed, while the others, the faceless ones, came and went.

The stabilization gradually gave faces and names to others as well, initially to the older Kapos and foremen, but then to other "Specialists" too. The Court Jew armband became superfluous, even bothersome. Kiewe, with his experience as a police chief, believed that it was not good to have the same people together for extended periods of time, and he did not approve of any unnecessary display, the kind of thing Franz, "the Doll," was quite fond of.

There is one other significant point about the Court Jews: in the eyes and ears of those who grew to have faces and names, and also had feet and hands made raw from toil, the expression *Court Jew* began to have a connotation as negative as that of *lepszy gocs,* "better guest." These days, *Court Jew* refers to those Jewish laborers from the lower part of the camp, just outside of the living quarters of the SS and the guards, the ones from the ghetto, from the workshops, from the kitchen, from the garage and the big depository too.

There are a few here, until now the only ones, who have been allowed to work in contact with nature, to see the camp of death from the outside, to distance themselves for a time from the smell of corpses that permeates everything—your lungs, the wood the barracks are built of. In those moments when they are driven out of the camp and into the forest, when they break branches off pine trees and collect them, they can get a whiff of life. But in the camouflage commando they only keep workers who are fit enough to climb high up into the trees and trot back to camp carrying heavy bundles of branches. They weave these branches into strands of barbed wire, thus maintaining the camouflage green around the entire perimeter of the camp.

Kurland, Kapo of the infirmary men, the smallest commando unit in the entire camp, is the oldest gravedigger, considering both his age and his service age here in Treblinka. Looking out over small round lenses in metal frames are eyes that must have seen a lot and have come to understand a lot. His nose is somewhat bulbous, a few of his teeth are missing, his cheeks are sunken, and his face seems to have been colored by the sand that has been burned dark and mixed with ashes. The whip that hangs from his belt always seems to be getting in his way: somehow it gets between his legs, which are clothed in pants made of a coarse material, and felt boots. And since he is of such small stature, the end of the thing drags across the floor. I believe that he must have been wearing his cap—which is also made of a coarse material and has a visor and ear flaps—when he came to Treblinka. In the few instances he takes the cap off to air it out, you can see a graying lock of hair. As a Kapo he has the privilege of not having to have his head shaved. Kapo Kurland spends his nights in the ghetto barracks with us, the Jewish workers, and his days in a small room in the "infirmary," when there are no transports coming. The SS drop in to chat, they say. I have never seen them lift a hand against him. None of the toughs in the meal line in front of the mess ever jostle him, not even by accident. They are more likely to get out of his way. He and his two assistants, neither of whom is all that young anymore, work exclusively with fire and with death.

And their powerful odor separates them from the others in this part of the camp, who by comparison are very minor gravediggers. Kapo Kurland probably came to be assigned to the "infirmary" because at the time the first transports were arriving and being scrutinized, he told the SS that outside in life he was what is known here as an army surgeon.

Camp Elder Galewski is, or was, an engineer by profession. Here he is the aristocratic speaker for the slaves of Treblinka. He's probably in his forties. His shoulders are bent slightly forward, as is often the case with tall people. His black hair, graying at the temples and combed smoothly back, makes his face look even thinner. With his bent nose, looking more noble than Jewish, and his fine black mustache, he is for SS tastes an impressive figure. The SS could not accept someone like the grumbler and blusterer Rakowski, with his round, somewhat feminine face, and of course no one like a Talmudist or a thief from the Jewish underground in Warsaw. The camp elder had to be someone whom they wouldn't immediately be tempted to beat up. Galewski understands the fate and the duties of those who are selected to work in Treblinka.

With a correct bearing he clicks the heels of his brightly polished boots together and speaks an acceptable German. He is also polite to us, when he urges rather than orders us to do something, always in Polish. Even though he understands Yiddish, he cannot speak it. He almost never gets angry, except at ruthless cheats, when there is hunger or a scarcity of water, for example.

How can you tell that you have become someone important in Treblinka, that you have a face and a name? Simply by how easy it is for you to get through a workshop in the evening, especially the tailor shop, and into "society." Not everyone is allowed in during his free time, before nine o'clock, to play at having a life. There are crowds at the door. Swearing and cursing give way to fistfights that no one wins—not even those who separate the combatants. On the inside there are discussions and a warm stove too, now that winter has begun. Little Edek plays his accordion, redheaded Schermann plays the violin, and Salwe sings. The others stand around the workshop tables. Sometimes a few of the women join in. It is said that, here and there, a few even find moments in which to satisfy their most personal desires. I find this hard to believe. In Treblinka these feelings are the first to be burned out, even before the rest of our bodies. Anyway, where would people get together now that the women are living in separate quarters? Wherever you go, wherever you are, you are nothing but one element in a cacophonous throng. There is no quiet in Treblinka. No one is ever alone, no one.

A Little Something in Your Pocket

Even before I had worked my way a couple of meters forward in the long line at the kitchen door, night fell, one of those winter nights illuminated by stars and a snowless frost. Tall rectangles of pale light shine from the doors of the kitchen and the barracks, the bright piercing shaft of a searchlight burns over the entrance to the ghetto, and lamplight from the SS quarters flickers through the trees. I look behind me into the frosty heights over the death camp and watch the deep red glow separating into a spectrum of colors I have never seen before: orange, yellows, deep purple, green purple, sulphurous haze.

In my cracked bowl, two unpeeled potatoes and some peelings are floating around in about a half liter of thickened liquid. The bowl burns my fingers. I walk away carefully to avoid the crush of bodies. Good God, just don't let this bowl be knocked out of my hands now. You are everything I have, you are all I have to lay out on my bunk, you, my life . . .

Getting ready for bed always brings with it an attempt at delousing, by hand and always in vain. The more clothes we wear to protect ourselves against the winter cold, the more lice we hatch. The fewer clothes we wear, the more we feel the bite of the winter frost.

Robert, already dressed for the night, is bouncing around on his bunk. Underneath a thick sweater, right up against his skin, he is wearing a long nightgown made of silk, a fabric difficult for the lice to cling to. To protect his bare shaved head from the icy night air, he is wearing a nightcap, which he has knotted together from a piece of silk stocking. While the rest of us are putting on similar dress, Robert is misting himself from a perfume bottle filled with something assumed to be disinfectant. Some babe must have brought the atomizer. It was made of cut glass. Or maybe, just like Robert, its previous owner had already put it to this alien use.

"Achtung!" sounds a voice through the barracks door. On top bunks and lower bunks, we all leap up, stand stiffly at attention, and show our "respect" to the SS and the guards looking in on us in our long flowing gowns made of pink, bright blue, and yellow flannel, woolen women's nightdresses, long underwear generously stuffed, topped off with nightcaps and hand warmers—ghosts, jumping jacks, scarecrows.

After the parade we curl up in our blankets and quietly carry on a debate about Kuba, our barracks elder, whom everyone is starting to view with suspicion. Hans has the last word: "For me, it's enough proof when I see the guy chewing on something every night before he goes to sleep. In these hungry times, we've got to keep an eye on anyone who's using his jaws more than the rest of us are."

We get up in the morning in a damp mist saturated with the nighttime breath and perspiration of the 350 men in the barracks. The dampness clings to the walls and the dirt floors. Our blankets and clothing are soaked, sticky, and wet. Heavy drops hanging from the overhead beams are released and fall onto the bunks. When the doors to the barracks open, clouds of condensation roll out into the frigid gray morning.

"*No, kurwa twoja matj*—you sonofabitch." The curse is aimed at the guy in the top bunk who, while making his bed, has just shaken his blanket out right in your face.

"*Do cholery jasnej*—pure cholera." Someone loses his balance while pulling on his boots and takes two others down with him. "Heniek, *Prosze tebe*—I beg you, get up, you've got to, get hold of yourself!" Someone is prodding his feverish comrade. "*Hab ka Kojach*—I don't have any more strength." The answer, in Yiddish, is swallowed up by other voices.

"*Du Schwein*." Rudi is angry, hanging by his hands from the overhead beams, his body swinging over the bunks. "You have to piss in the pot when it's already overflowing with shit? That can—" and he's interrupted: "Oh, oh, buddy, what are we going to catch here in Treblinka?" Arms fly into the air, pants fall, and more bare asses join in the crazy laughter.

"Thou hast watched over me during this night, Almighty, and

hast shown me the light of a new day—hallowed be thy Name." For morning prayer, he has wound the phylacteries around his arms and all the way up to his forehead. He is banging his head rhythmically against the top bunk, just under my feet. Maybe he is one of the "holy men" here, who has begun to believe that Hitler will save us from all sins, that he is the messiah who will gather all Jews together in one place—in Treblinka?

At morning roll call, Kiewe, dressed in his long military coat with its ample fur collar, his breath visible in the cold air, announces: "There will be a transport arriving today. Everything from the transport, all foodstuffs, will be brought to the warehouse. And let me tell you," his voice breaking into a screech, "anyone caught with that food, anyone caught speculating, will suffer the consequences!"

Speculating, speculation—these words are as common here as *infirmary* or *bath*. They came from the outside, from life, and are distorted here in Treblinka, like everything else. *Speculating* means secretly taking things, grabbing, looting, and smuggling food, clothing, money, gold, for your group, for yourself, for trade. Now, in these hungry days the little camp man Beniek, who is not allowed up on the sorting site, will trade a pot full of barley for a pair of boots from the store. The guys from the carpentry shop secretly cook it and get to keep half of it for their trouble. For a deftly deposited roll of banknotes, *dobry pan Wachmann*—our dear Mr. Guard will provide, just as stealthily, a piece of white bread, some sausage, a small bottle of vodka, and a few Machorkova cigarettes, everything wrapped up in brown paper. We all have to speculate in order to hold on, *tryzymal sie*, to endure.

Not a single flake of snow has fallen, but still the sorting site is completely white. Hoarfrost covers the barrack roofs and dusts the green fencing that encloses the camp and divides it into blocks like large pens at a slaughterhouse. By the time we get up to Barracks A, on the double, Zelo has frozen white droplets on his mustache. According to the thermometer at the entrance to the barracks, it's minus twenty-three degrees Fahrenheit.

After a prolonged whistle, we can hear the cars arriving, squealing even more loudly than usual. Now it is almost certain that there will be no SS coming into the barracks. Most of them are out on the platform waiting for the transport to come in, or at the disrobing site overseeing the operation. I climb up on the stacks of bundled and sorted coats, way up to the top to the wooden wall that separates us from the station. Meanwhile Karl is on lookout below. Through a crack in the wall I see a cattle car encrusted with ice. Pairs of eyes, crowded one upon another, are staring out from a small barred window.

One of the Blues begins tugging on the iron bolt of the door. But he can't get it open. Curses, and the whip flies out at his head several times—but I don't see the two arms in uniform. The Blue disappears and then returns with a hammer. He pounds the frozen lock open from below, while the whips continue to crack. It appears to be some kind of strange mechanism, where each crack of the whip is translated into a blow of the hammer. Finally the lock is opened, but the door is stuck. It can't be budged. Another Blue comes running up with something that looks like a sledgehammer. Again, in time with the whips, he pounds the frame of the door until it comes free, at first just slightly, then more. An awful tangled mass pours out of the black opening. In no time the platform is filled with people carrying backpacks, sacks, and bundles of blankets. Pots are rolling around on the slippery and icy ground.

A woman and two men are lying close to the door. They don't appear to be quite dead, but others are already falling over them, and in turn others from farther back in the car are tripping over them. Packs come tumbling down. An old woman falls on her face, doesn't get up; all she can do is raise her head a few times. Someone trips over her, and her skirt gets pulled up. She's covered with excrement, probably has dysentery—I've seen that before.

A boy, probably about twelve years old, stops at the door, his eyes staring out from under a cap pulled down over his ears. Something is pulling him down to the ground, and as he bends forward he's being held back by his coattails, which have become entangled somewhere between the sliding door and the wall of the cattle car. The boy disappears, falling through the narrow gap between the car and the platform. The only thing now visible is a part of his coat held taut by the weight of his body hanging somewhere beneath the platform.

A tall young man staggers out, followed by a woman. He is bareheaded, his long hair disheveled, with a stubbly beard on his face. His long coat hangs slack on his body; all the buttons have been torn off. He has a dark patch of blood under one ear, worn gray felt boots on his feet. He's carrying a bundle in each hand. The woman following him unfortunately steps on the head of one of the bodies lying on the floor. She loses her footing, and as she's reaching for support, she knocks one of the bundles out of his hand. The bundle breaks open, and their miserable hoard rolls out onto the platform: potatoes, a pot containing a small piece of margarine, rolled-up linens, grubby little cloth bags, half full, wrinkled, probably containing food. The man turns around, takes the woman by the arm, and pulls her up. Then he bends over again under the blows from Kiewe's whip. They weren't moving fast enough. The second bundle also falls to the ground. The man's face is smeared with blood, but the blood isn't running. It is so cold that the blood has frozen into dark red stripes and clots. The man is trying to protect the woman from the whip with his own body. He doesn't want to let her go, and now he is gathering himself as if to resist. Kiewe is overflowing with rage. Sepp Hirtreiter jumps in from the other side to provide assistance and delivers two murderous blows. They all disappear from my view.

The man had a yellow star sewn onto the front of his coat on the left side and another one on the back. That means that this is a transport from occupied Soviet territory. That's how Jews are identified there. Jews from Poland wear a white armband with a blue Star of David. Jews arriving in transports from Theresienstadt wear the well-known yellow star on the left side of their chests; these stars are inscribed with the word *Jude*—an indication that the wearers are European Jews.

The commotion and screaming on the platform fade away. The last people stagger out of the cars and gasp for breath. Not a single suitcase or real backpack—just bags, bundles, and sacks with cords sewn on so they can be carried on one's back. It's enough to tell me that this is a miserably poor transport from somewhere to the east.

"Down now," David Brat whispers into my ear. He's been right next to me watching everything. "They'll be driving us out onto the platform to clean things up, and you can bet that every car in this transport will be full of . . ." Warning signals shoot through the barracks from box to box.

First of all, dead and motionless bodies will have to be carried out of each of the cars onto the platform. I pull my cap down over my ears, run into the first car, grab a couple of legs and pull, but it doesn't work. The body to which the two legs are attached is weighed down with other bodies. I take hold of two thin female legs. The coarse stockings crack in my hands. They must have been completely soaked. Then back into the car again. Now, on top there's a dead body with a slit throat. The head is hanging down off the back. This is the work of Ukrainian thugs in the ghettos. I think I'll take hold of some other free hand, but then I let it drop. I can see that if I held on more tightly and pulled, it would come off. I go back to the body with the slit throat. At that moment Boelitz, wearing a fur hat instead of his usual field cap, takes up a position at the door and looks into the car.

The cars have finally been emptied. And now we grab the blankets we'll be using to carry the dead bodies to the "infirmary." Karl, David Brat, Lublink, and I carry one blanket together, each of us holding an edge. All the bodies are lying there lined up so neatly along the entire length of the platform, their feet toward the wall of the barracks and their heads toward the cars. They no longer look so horrible. They are lumps. Handle them like lumps. The moment you look at any one of them as an individual, you're lost. No, you can't do that; you can never not look. The motionless eyes—I always get caught, cannot escape them, I get trapped, there are eyes everywhere, all of them staring at me, getting larger and larger, already blocking out foreheads, entire faces, resting on chins . . . Stop, not like this—okay, look, look right at them as if this whole thing were intensely interesting, as if you were investigating every detail, every single body. How many dead bodies are there anyway? One a waxy yellow, one emaciated, one bloated and unimaginably heavy, covered with small deep purple bullet holes and odd bright puncture wounds. It's interesting, fascinating, terribly interesting . . .

How many loads have I carried to the "infirmary," and how many times have I returned to the platform? And the next one is some old man, wearing nothing more than a long shirt, a collection of bones sheathed in skin, covered with huge white spots. I can easily wrap my fingers around his ankles. As we lift up the blanket, something begins to move. Marshaling every bit of strength she has, a woman, probably middle-aged, sits up. Her undone hair is matted, her entire face smudged and grimy. The expression in her eyes is the worst thing . . . "Mad," I hear Lublink's strained voice.

We lift the blanket with the dead old man. He is as light as a feather. The woman's upper body falls back over again. Her legs are covered with bundles and other items left behind. Kapo Rakowski's powerful voice carries up from the lower field: "Faster with those corpses, fa-a-a-ster, come on . . ." There is a jar of *Schmalz* or something of the sort lying on the ground. A number of us run by with our blankets—and the jar disappears in the commotion.

We come running into the "infirmary." The old man in the long shirt flies through the air in a great arc, falls into the pit, and disappears in the flames, which at their tips turn green and violet in the icy air. On the glittering icy ramparts above, a guard in a fur coat reaching down to his ankles, the collar turned up, stamps his feet to keep himself warm. As we turn to go back, the next bearers are already propelling their load into the air: "Ho-oh-oh-upp!"

The body with the long hair flies through the air. It's the mad woman from the train car. David Brat takes a step forward, still holding the edge of the blanket in his right hand and reaching out with the left, his lips open wide enough to show his protruding front teeth: "Nahh, she isn't . . ." Terrible screams pierce through the bedlam. Down among the flames something can be seen rising ever so slightly—

"What are you hanging around and shouting about? Get outta here!" Miete spins around and takes aim at us, his legs spread, his cap pushed back further on his head than usual, his pallid face red, as if it had been boiled, but his eyes as glassy as ever.

"Did you see the kid with that bloated belly and face?" gasped David Brat, once we were back in the barracks. "Do you know why that happens? You don't know? That's starvation, a phase of starvation. When a transport leaves the ghetto, it first goes into quarantine—anyway, that's what they call it—and that's where the shooting and the killing start. Maybe that's where the kid lost his parents. And who could take care of him, when you don't even have the strength to take care of your own?" David grabs me by the shoulder with his bony fingers. A sad, understanding smile begins to show through his sturdy teeth. "Richard, my boy, you don't know—none of you know . . . Until now you guys from Theresienstadt have been treated like aristocracy. You arrived on passenger trains. For us, Treblinka starts in the ghettos. And almost everyone helps in some way to get rid of the Jews. Or at least they have in some way assented . . ."

Little Abraham is bringing in a load of women's coats to be sorted, somehow a little too quickly. Hans stands up and looks around: "Hey, why such a hurry? What's under those coats?" He digs into the pile of coats with his foot until he finds what he's expecting to find on the very bottom: "Hey, Abraham, you pig, can't you at least wait until the owner of that bag is dead!"

Abraham is already kneeling over the bundle hidden by the coats. He's already got his hands in the bag. To anyone looking in from the outside, he simply appears to be rummaging through the coats. But all the while he's watching everything, just like Hans, and from time to time he looks up at Hans, a little ashamed, a little apologetic, and answers: "It doesn't matter, Hans, now or later. I'm gonna die too, worse than this bag's owner."

Grabbing on to a railing, Hans leans out of his box into ours: "If I smack him one now, I won't know if it's for the dead woman or for that piece of bacon he's just found in her bag."

From the other end of the barracks Zelo is chasing after another bearer with a similarly suspicious-looking armful of coats. This is the first time we've ever seen Zelo use his whip. Kiewe, appearing at the far end of the barracks near the entrance, just watches as the two of them pass by our boxes and turn to go out, and then he yells enthusiastically: "Yeah, Zelo, that's the way. Let 'em have it, let 'em really have it!"

Zelo turns around and comes back to our boxes, his eyes watering, maybe because of the cold, maybe out of shame and outrage: "Someone from that last transport, he grabbed it right out of his hands . . ."

"Well, well." David's pal, Lublink, walks toward us from his box across the way, a brownish face, sharp features, a little stooped from all the drudgery. "I don't know this guy. He's probably a real pig. But that boy over there by the stack of pants"—pointing with his hand and raising a single fused clump of eyebrow—"I know him. He's a neighbor, and I know he never saw this much food at home, and out there in life he never stuffed himself as full as he's stuffing himself here in Treblinka. Not that his family was really poor, but his papa was damned tight, saving up to emigrate, to America, to Palestine. Away from Poland. For this he bought dollars and diamonds . . ."

Again we hear steam whistles and the squeal of more wheels.

More cars are at the platform. These cars are emptied too. Suddenly, as I am removing the last of the bundles and whatever else remains, the figures of Boelitz, Bredow, and others again fill the platform across its entire width: "Kapo of the Red commando, here, put these men to work getting rid of these clothes and all this other stuff . . ." And I know that this means we'll be carrying off the clothes from the disrobing site and from the barracks where the women have undressed. There are lots of things lying around. And the Reds can't get the job done fast enough.

They herd us right into the barracks. Usually, looking from a corner past piles of clothing, I can see the last of the naked backs as they head for the "hairdressers." But today the barracks are still full. Into half of the building, along one entire wall, naked bodies are pressed together—an enormous mural, a fresco of bottoms, bellies, arms folded over breasts, undone hair. Along the opposite wall are piles of clothing, some smaller, some larger. The body odor clogs your nose and your mouth and stings your eyes. The screams of children pierce through the bedlam into your ears.

"Hey, you," one of the Red thugs jars me out of my crippling daze and points me at my work. As I slowly bend over the clothes, my eyes still staring straight ahead, he winks, leans over to me, and yells into my ear in Polish, very slowly and clearly, to be sure I understand: "Well, well, has one of your dreams from out there in life come true, seeing a whole roomful of naked broads? *Ruszaj sie, jazda*—getta move on, and keep movin'!"

The platform is filled six more times, and each time, after everyone who can still stand on two feet has left, there's the same sight—rags, skeletons sheathed in skin, dead and dying. By early afternoon the entire transport has been processed—more than five thousand people.

It would be pointless to sort coats from these miserable transports according to quality. So we process the coats, everyone from both work teams, Men's Coats Type I and Men's Coats Type II. Together we sort everything we get. I carefully remove the Jewish star from a short winter coat that has already been examined—here it's called a *kurtka*—and set it aside. The little white strings in the quilted lining are moving almost imperceptibly. They are rows of slow crawling lice.

Willinger, who only appears to be clumsy, grabs the *kurtka* and feels through it again, then tears it open at the shoulder and pulls five twenty-dollar bills out of the quilted lining. Although it is mainly his strength we are counting on for our coming escape, Willinger, for all his simpleness, also has what is known as a Jewish nose. His actual nose, sitting over his mustache, is remarkably pointed. But what we're referring to here is a special talent, a heightened sensitivity. Willinger fixes his gaze on a pair of children's shoes. Something has caught his attention. He gets up, goes over to the shoes, and tears off the heel, thereby exposing a twenty-dollar gold piece. Next, his small searching eyes are attracted to a belt, grimy and worn. None of us would have any use for it. He begins to squeeze the belt with his thick fingers, ripping open the seams until several coins are exposed—five- and ten-ruble gold pieces. Willinger senses the admiration he has aroused, basks in his eminence, and would prefer to inspect and sort the entire plunder himself. And in a show of superior physical strength— *"Nie, nie*—no, no, let me do it"—he lifts the bundle of sorted coats off my shoulder and with just one hand tosses it up on top of the stacked coats in my box. "*Wy chlopacy*—you boys, save your strength." He's looking at Karl and me. "You'll need it, you're worth it . . ." At first I freeze, and then I want to scream in shame. This giant of a man from somewhere out in Czenstochau thinks we're somehow better—like children who must be saved. Of our kind we must endure . . .

Meanwhile Willinger has fished another glittering object out of the lining of a coat. He shows it to us furtively and hurriedly explains: "This thing's probably six carats, Karol." He leans over to Karl, somehow very gently: "Why bother with a house, a piece of land? For us, something you can just pick up and take with you. A little something in your pocket, right."

❋

Typhus versus Plan H

After the transports from the east, supposedly from Grodno and
Białystok too, there is again a long period of inactivity at the
station. The cold tapers off, the hunger grows, and lice still contami-
nate all of Treblinka.

Zelo comes to our box to inspect the hiding place we have built
using stacks of sorted coats. A few bundles from the middle stack
have been removed to create a big cavity surrounded on all sides by
bundles of coats. There are also bundles over the top of the hollow
space. "This way we can get three or four people in here," Karl
thinks, "and if we're ordered to move these things, or something like
that, we can just collapse the whole thing with coats."

Recently, for short intervals, this is where we've been hiding a few
people who've come down with a strange fever. But pretty soon it
will be used for its intended purpose in our grand plan for Treblinka.
No more single escapes, no "ten shot for every one who escapes," as
Lalka has declared, but all of us, together . . .

During the winter most of the work has been transferred to the
barracks. The SS do not make regular rounds, but we have observed
that, at certain intervals, they alternately pass through the barracks
up at the sorting site and then go down to the workshops.

The time best suited to our purposes seems to be between three
and four in the afternoon, when there is a changing of the guard—
presumably for coffee.

"And at this H hour, a few dependable men will take up positions
at the entrance to each of the barracks." Zelo lays out the plan he has
developed with Camp Elder Galewski, Kapo Kurland from the
"infirmary," engineer Sudowicz from the construction commando,
as well as a few others down at the workshops. "Anyone may come
in, but not a single soul may leave, except for certain messengers. As

soon as anyone in uniform enters the barracks, you will put a coat over his head and strangle him with a cord. No knife wounds, no struggle, no blood, because they'll be coming in one right after the other."

"And what if more than one of them happens to invade?" a voice comes from one of the boxes.

"You all know yourselves that it would be highly unusual for six of them to come in together. But even if they did, they'd be handled the same way. We believe that in all probability no more than three of them will show up at one time. That's why we'll assign ten designated people to each entrance, and we will also have reserves. There should always be three men to handle one uniform, as they come in. If two of them should happen to come in together and walk along side by side, then the one with the higher rank will belong to the first three men. Those of you next to the entrance can drag them to our hiding place in the stack of coats and finish them off there with the cords we use to tie these bundles. This is what we'll have to be doing in each of the barracks during this hour. Then, with the weapons we take from them, we will storm headquarters and the ammunition store, immediately setting everything on fire . . ."

Our discussion is interrupted by the arrival of the kitchen detail. Now, in winter, we work without breaking for lunch. Food is brought to us in the work buildings to our workplaces—buckets full of ersatz coffee and bread in a bedsheet, already sliced into individual portions. Eyes search for the biggest piece, carefully observing hands as they distribute the slices, the entire procession stopping one by one at each individual box. From your own portion your eyes glide on to the portion of the second man and the third, and then on to the serving for the next box. You compare.

The debate on Plan H will be continued that evening in the carpentry shop with Simcha. Simcha is sitting on one of the workbenches, swinging his crossed legs back and forth, his hands folded in his lap. They are worker's hands with short, broad thumbs. Simcha had not chosen the wrong profession at Treblinka. Simcha was a trained cabinetmaker. In general I am surprised at how many of them are craftsmen. At our site most of us are business people, accountants, people with a university education. Here many of them are tailors, shoemakers, and goldsmiths. But there are some bankers too: Alexander, for example, Kapo of the Gold Jew commando.

"Oh well, dying—it's just that first we all see ourselves hanging naked by our ankles, head down," I can hear them say as I begin to become more involved in the discussion.

Simcha sits up a little straighter and shoves his chest forward. He is exceptionally strong given his small stature. The shaved head atop his thick neck has turned completely black from thick stubble. Below that is his dark brown face. His low forehead has two pronounced furrows, and thick black eyebrows grow together at the top of his small snub nose. "I've decided I'm going to stay in Treblinka. I want to stay with my people over there, take revenge for them, and show the world." Simcha seems really to be talking to himself now, trying to convince himself that he has no other choice. "I will always know that this wood is not the same as the wood I worked with in life on the outside, that here every piece is like a dead man over there, that I'll always be cutting nothing but nearly dead men, sawing . . ."

"In any case, we have to know more about what's going to happen in the SS barracks and at headquarters," Zelo continues. "Is there really a call from Malkinia every hour, and what kind of telegraph do they have . . ."

"And what's going to happen in the second camp?" Simcha asks.

"That's just it. We'll have to split up and attack headquarters and the second camp at the same time. We'll have to carry out our plan in Camp 1 and then head over there. We're certainly better off here than they are over there. The mood among the Ukrainians . . ."

"You never know what they'll do," adds Simcha.

"It's possible that they'll just run off without a shot, once they see that we've jumped the SS. But it's more likely they'll fight like mad. They know that they'll never have it better than they've got it in Treblinka. And even all the bribery. Their pockets are full of money, gold, and jewelry. Supposedly they're burying it in the woods. It's obvious that they'll never get enough. It's just that they take piles of money and gold from you, make promises, and then betray you in serenely good conscience, actually with no conscience at all."

For the next few days, following evening roll call, Zelo immediately goes to talk to Galewski and Kurland, and even our visitors in the bunks alternate. We'll need gasoline, and that means Standa

Lichtblau. He works in the garage. Of all of us, the twenty Czechoslovakians in the camp, he has built the "most successful career" at Treblinka. He was an automobile mechanic in Moravian Ostrów, and in his case the SS made a really fortunate selection. No one knows as much about trucks as he does. And that's why he's never mistreated by his supervisor, Sergeant Schmidt. Standa enjoys a privileged status.

This time, up on the bunk, he claims he's come to see Robert to get some kind of ointment, but he's talking to Zelo. His physique is similar to Simcha's, but otherwise he's quite different. He doesn't have such a sturdy build, and instead of dark skin the stocky Standa has pink cheeks and a smile on his face. You can't tell whether he's happy or sad. He nods to Zelo, and as he leaves, he says: "Even the extra ration of soup they give me from the Ukrainian mess won't stop me."

Meanwhile Robert has filled his atomizer with disinfectant. Now he turns to Zelo, who quickly nods, indicating to Robert that Karl and Hans have already left the upper bunks and that he must also leave if we are to be able to settle down to sleep. But this time Robert loses his quiet tone of voice. He stands at the head of the bunk, his childlike face raised over the edge, and moves to the attack: "Wait, you idiots, and stop shaking your dirt in my face! Don't you see that we've gotten to the point where we do everything of our own accord? That they don't even have to beat us anymore? They've trained us, and we just about take care of the transports ourselves, while they just stand around and watch. Miete and Mentz are about the only ones left who do anything, parading into the infirmary for a little sharpshooting."

The next morning at roll call twelve men report in sick, the day after that sixteen, until the so-called Jewish sick bay is full of fevered patients. Even our hiding place under the piles of coats is full—and not the way we had intended. In the following weeks every third man, and then every second man, is dragging himself around with a 104-degree fever. It's typhus.

Robert says there are several different kinds of typhus. In Treblinka we've got a somewhat less severe form of the illness, but it's accompanied by a high fever nonetheless. Among ourselves we don't say that someone's got typhus; we say he's got "Treblinka." You don't catch it directly from another person. The infection is spread by lice. These lice thrive in unsanitary conditions, especially in clothing that cannot be properly washed at high temperatures.

The illness begins with a fever that quickly exceeds 104 degrees Fahrenheit. Of course we all drag ourselves around, trying to duck the disease, taking refuge in our hiding place until we can no longer hold out. It's only then that we stagger into the sick bay, to Dr. Rybak. There is never a free bed. The sick bay can normally accommodate about twenty people. But now there are more than thirty crammed into that very small space.

"Come back in two or three days" is Rybak's usual advice. That means going back into the struggle for a hiding place, especially to keep out of sight from the all-observant Miete. For how long? Until there's a free bed, until Rybak discharges someone from the sick bay or Miete has someone carried off to the "infirmary." And then, if the aspirant has not already collapsed from exhaustion or been dragged right off the work site, if he still has a claim and is deemed able to contribute to the "common cause," he will finally be admitted to the sick bay. Then he will lie there in unimaginable filth, thinking of nothing, or no one else, but Miete. The Angel of Death comes every day, sometimes with Kiewe. Rybak is required to report all serious cases to them. The sick bay office is like a vessel that must not be allowed to overflow. Those who are deemed hopeless are injected with some sort of an anesthetic and are carried off to the "infirmary." Strangely enough, Dr. Rybak has medical supplies here, some taken from the transports and some he has been able to acquire through speculative channels. Besides the infirmary injections for the hopeless, Dr. Rybak also gives various shots meant to strengthen the hopeful. But no one can be convinced that Rybak, dressed in his soiled white coat, needle in hand, intends to give them anything but an infirmary injection.

The eighth and the ninth days are critical. Lean, active men seem to recover from the illness most easily, while slow, heavier-set people have a more difficult time. According to Robert, who works as Rybak's assistant, the chief complications of the disease are pneumonia, meningitis, and just plain madness.

As February gives way to March, the days grow longer, and the weather milder. We again start getting our midday meal down at the mess. We use our short noontime break to check up on people who are still in the sick bay. The sick bay is about five meters wide and is located between the Jewish mess and a sleeping and living area. It shares an entrance with these barracks. The actual entrance is nothing more than a curtain made of blankets. There is a table with medical instruments off to the side of the small window, and beyond the table there is an alcove made of rough boards simply nailed together. In this alcove there is a sofa sprouting horsehair, and on the walls are two shelves. This is the doctor's office. Above it is something that looks like a kind of chicken coop and serves as Dr. Rybak's living quarters. The alcove is lined horizontally with boards, which form both the ceiling of the office and the floor of Rybak's room. The carpenters have also hammered together a ladder so that the good doctor can climb up into his sitting room and to his bed.

Leading away from the window, through the full length of the building, there is a narrow passageway between two rows of double bunks. My face and chest are suffused with the odor of feverish bodies, smells from the nearby kitchen, and the musty scent of wood. There is very little light coming through the small window, barely enough to distinguish the remains of food and vomit, bloody smudges from squashed fleas and lice on blankets that were once red, yellow, or green.

Bearded, forlorn faces, half-open mouths with lips spread taut, protruding jawbones, eyes pulled open wide in an empty stare, confused words and screams—this is Dr. Rybak's workplace. He works here every day and—unlike the rest of us—every night. Whenever one of his patients leaves the sickbed under his own power and reaches out his hand in thanks, Rybak, the doctor from Warsaw and onetime student at the University of Prague, often responds: "Don't thank me. Curse me. I'm not giving your life back to you. I'm returning you to all the terrible suffering of Treblinka."

When we arrived in Treblinka, Eugen Back, "the Eiffel Tower," was unquestionably the tallest man among us. He was a good two meters tall. We all felt like dwarfs when he marched in our row, always letting his head hang slightly to one side, with his longish freckled face. "Hopeless" is what Rybak told us as he came in. The doctor ran his hand back over his straight black hair, which he had been allowed to keep long, and his broad face became even broader.

That afternoon Eugen suffered fits. He tore off the straps that the Reds—who had been called in to help—had used to tie him down. Then, having been given an infirmary injection, he simply lay there motionless.

Through the open entryway at the far end of Barracks A, directly facing our stall, we can see a passageway, as if it were framed in a stage set; it leads from the sorting site to the "infirmary." This afternoon the Reds have carried their litters across the stage eight times. Miete always follows after them with his rolling gait. Franz, "the Doll," and Bredow stand around watching the processions pass by, gently tapping the tops of their boots with their whips. After one shot the litter always returns empty. Now, from under a blanket, the next body is hanging out over both ends of the litter, head uncovered, chin protruding into the air.

We wait until we hear the shot, and then Hans starts working on a coat. "Well, he won't be going back home to Prague the way he always wanted, wearing his own boots, the ones he was wearing when he came, the ones he ran around in, as worn out as they were. In all those piles of shoes he couldn't find any others that would fit him. He wore size thirteen, and they didn't send any other Jews here with size thirteen."

Kiewe bursts into the work barracks so suddenly that he gets to us before the warning signals do. He spots one of us weakened by fever, leaning up against a stack of bundled coats. He whips the man across the face until it's covered with blood, then he races through the whole building lashing out, and from the other end of the barracks I hear him raging at Zelo, that the entire Barracks A is loafing, the best team of workers has become nothing but a pack of malingerers. Screaming his threat "I'll get you!" he races out.

After evening roll call, as Kiewe enters his report and then closes his journal, we get the order: "Camp 1 dismissed, except for Barracks A. Because of outrageous loafing and malingering, all occupants of Barracks A will be subject to penalty drills!" Kiewe spits out each individual word. "Foremen and Kapos will be exempt. I am assuming their duties. *Achtung*—in threes—double time, march!"

Karl, redheaded Jojne, and I form the first troika at the head of the line. No one had wanted to go first. But it turns out to be an advantage. When Kiewe interrupts the run with the orders "Down—

up," we have open space in front of us. The men behind us are getting in each other's way, tripping over each other. They can't keep
up, and the whips beat them to the ground.

This new spectacle is attracting the attention of other SS men.
Before long, the crack of the whip is setting the tempo we follow as
we are herded around the assembly site. Off in one corner, Lalka is
simply observing the action without taking part, perhaps chagrined
that he, Master Sergeant Kurt Franz, is not directing this scene himself. Outside, in normal life, this would be a routine exercise for athletes and soldiers. For men in Treblinka, suffering from "Treblinka,"
it is a death march.

"Whoever takes off a single piece of clothing is gonna get it. Keep
your interval—keep your interval, you bastard!" and then we hear
the whip crack. These SS men, these Germans, drilled in military
precision, can be brought to a frenzy by anyone who shows an
inability to move in a disciplined and orderly way. By the way he's
hobbling around instead of doing double time, it looks as if our
Mosche, from somewhere in Rembertów, is making fun of the whole
drill.

Once in the curve, I have an overview of the entire field. There
are only a few rows in which men are still running in formation. Men
with greater endurance have moved into the front ranks in place of
those who have fallen back or fallen out. Six men are standing side
by side, leaning against the wall of the barracks, exhausted. Among
them is sixteen-year-old Hans Burg. He was released yesterday, following his worst day in the sick bay. The bloody foam around his
half-opened mouth is being washed away by the blood flowing out
of his nose. The other faces are all the same: the eyes of hunted men
stare out from the reddish black smear of blood and cinders from the
assembly site. Meanwhile a savage chase is under way. With whips
cracking, the SS cull individual men from the group and drive them
across the field to the others at the barracks wall. Miete is standing
near them, near the fallen men. He takes charge of them. Now they
belong to him, the Angel of Death. And even the Doll, Franz, is
putting in an appearance and participating. He just couldn't stay
away after all.

So this is what they are going to do with all of us. Slowly, so we
won't panic, man by man, they will sift through us, slowly, so that

each of us will believe he has a chance to be among those who will survive. And they will play the men off against their foremen.

"Halt—at ease—at rest—from now on this will be the punishment for loafers and malingerers. Dismissed, to your barracks without supper!" Küttner screams, putting an end to this torment. From the top bunk, pressed up against the small barred window, we watch them being taken away. Hans Burg, the youngest of the Czech group here . . .

And another one who is more boy than man. Kiewe determines his identity. His name is Maier, from the tag that for some time now each of the sorters has been required to put in with the bundles of coats he has sorted. When the bundles are loaded for shipment, the tags are removed. It's just a spot check, but a bull's-eye for Kiewe. Attached to a threadbare Woman's Coat Type II, which Kiewe has carried out to the middle of the sorting site and held high, there is a bright yellow star that should have been removed. It is a symbol of his fate, this youth from Warsaw, left for him by a woman who arrived on a transport carrying five thousand people from Grodno.

They hacked off the blond boyish curl on his forehead, and now they will hack away at all of his sixteen years. "As a warning he will be shot here on the spot in front of you all." Kiewe announces the new punishment after we have formed a half circle facing the sand ramparts surrounding the second camp. "Now strip," he says quietly to the boy, but loud enough for us to hear.

Now watch carefully. Now you will see close up exactly how a man is shot dead in front of many other men. You won't have an opportunity like this every day. The boy is slowly undressing. His one somewhat squinting eye, along with a slightly bowed nose and narrow, well-defined lips, gives him a rather impish look. But no, he's just taking his shirt off so he can wash his upper body. They're not going to shoot him . . . What could he have been thinking about when he picked up this coat? He sits down on the ground, half naked, looks to his right and to his left at the SS men who have closed the half circle, as if he wanted to ask them: "Shall I take my shoes off or not?" Sitting there with his legs folded, he makes several attempts to take off one boot or the other.

Stop, wait, stop. You're taking off your life! We'll all break out now, with our boots on our feet, trample . . . Who's going where? To which side? Miete serves up an imperious blow of the whip to one of our group. Oh no, don't wait for anything. We'll help you get your boots off. There, you see, the boots are already off. He doesn't cry, he doesn't beg like so many older ones before him. All he does is look around sorrowfully and wait, wait, until they graze his backside with their whips, smile, and say the same thing he heard so many times before on the outside, in life: "Now, that's so you won't do it again. Get your things together and get out . . ."

The grim winter sun makes its way over the rampart, and from in front of this immense, dark red disk, like a black-robed messenger, a bringer of evil slipping and sliding, a guard runs down the embankment, waving his rifle over his head: "Sergeant, sir, me, let me— shoot—let me . . ."

"Can you shoot straight?" I hear Miete ask him. The guard, a few years older than the condemned man, makes a confident gesture, and when Miete nods in agreement, he steps back, turned halfway toward us, still waving his weapon wildly over his head. He's laughing. He's happy. The dark-complected Ukrainian youth takes a few more steps back, then another step forward, at the same time seeking firm footing.

The victim is still rubbing his hands together. Looking into the muzzle of the gun, he squints even more with his left eye, raises his right eyebrow, and turns his head and his body to the side in order to elude what is going to be fired at him in the very next moment. Once more he steps back a little . . .

A shot—a small red spot appears on his chest. At the same time his body, arms sprawling, flies into the air and falls back onto the ground. The outstretched legs of his broken body fly apart and convulsively pull together again. Miete leans over him, lays his pistol directly on the boy's temple, and with two shots puts an end to the thrashing of legs. So now, in the greatest possible detail, you have again seen how life becomes death.

Miete and Küttner burst into the sick bay together. Kiewe asks Rybak if he really needs three people to take care of the sick, and Rybak responds, feebly, that two of them, Robert and another assistant, work during the day, and he himself works mainly at night. Küttner turns to Miete and says: "He seems interested in introducing something like a night shift." He decides that starting the next morning, Robert, "the pharmacist," will return to the task of sorting drugs in Barracks B.

There seems to be a definite purpose to Kiewe's intervention. There's something behind it. Until now, they've used general cleansing, winnowing, and workforce reduction in slow periods when supplies were scarce. The winter cold, hunger, and disease took care of the nastiest chores. The penalty drills at the assembly site were enough—now even Barracks B, the Reds, and the Blues are taking drills—and there were enough other punishments to ensure that the wheat was separated from the chaff. And when empty train cars arrived to be filled, this would suffice. For one, two, three days on end, men ran to the ramps laden with bundles and then back to the barracks, where sorted wares were piled up to the ceiling. With fevers as high as 104 degrees, they feigned good health, strength, and readiness to work. A few of them simply collapsed; a few were helped along by SS men and guards. The only good thing about this mad rush was that, when we fell into our bunks at night, we were no longer hungry. Several fully loaded freight cars left Treblinka every day. Destinations were written on the sides of the cars in chalk: Bremen, Aachen, Schweinfurt . . . As Hans Freund always said, "Everything to be disinfected upon arrival, postage paid."

The mountains outside, as well as the stacks in the barracks, are dwindling. Having no place to hide, no place to go without being observed, we pace around nervously behind the wooden slats of our empty boxes, like animals in a zoo. There are still a few bundles in the women's lingerie boxes, and men's underwear and suits, and in Box A, as it is called, there are even some stored bolts of fabric. This is apparently being kept for future use in the tailor shop.

Zelo is the first one of us forced to go to the sick bay, and he seems to have a particularly severe case of "Treblinka." But Kiewe decides in his favor: "Wel-l-ll, we can use this man," he says to Rybak as he makes one of the "super rounds." It's obvious that Robert's demotion and reassignment back up to the sorting site were due solely to Küttner's bad mood.

In a show of patriotic sentiment toward the few "hard-working boys from Bohemia" who had somehow landed among the "pack from Poland," Sergeant Suchomel—during the peacetime thirties, a tailor and member of a German-speaking minority in Bohemian

Krummau, and here the jovial head of the Gold Jew Commando—
has soup and oranges sent to Zelo from the German mess. Look
here, an orange—a genuine orange with a soft peel, no hint of rot,
still emitting scents of the wondrous outside world.

Everyone greets Zelo the first time he's back at the assembly site,
going back to work—our Zelo. "We'll have to set the slowest possible work tempo without getting you put on a death run." Zelo and
his colleague, Foreman Adasch, are going from one box to another.
We understand we'll gain about eight days this way. That is the
deadline for Plan H. Robert, now in the sick bay himself, will have
recovered by then. He has already survived the crisis.

Late in the afternoon Kiewe bursts into Barracks A like some
enormous piece of hot iron slag and has all sorted bundles counted,
thus ascertaining that there is a total of 132 bundles of men's shirts,
instead of the reported 205. Missing are 73 bundles of men's shirts,
packed ten to a bundle. There is a small pile of approximately twenty items yet to be sorted. Apart from these, there are no shirts in Treblinka, or sports jackets either.

Everyone in Barracks A knows how this most likely came about.
There have been no shirts of good quality for some time now. So
people started speculating with the ones that had already been sorted. They opened bundles that had already been processed and traded these goods for an extra portion of bread, or for a few cubes of
sugar from down at the workshops, from the kitchen. When the
jacket or shirt you are wearing gets dirty or is torn, you simply throw
it away onto a pile of rejects or directly into the fire. And the guys
have been reporting numbers to fulfill their daily quota without having actually done the work. There was nothing else they could do.
They were quivering from the high fevers of "Treblinka." Idiots—
they were waiting for the next transports to arrive, for new supplies,
so they could catch up again and bring everything back into line. In the
meantime they've messed up everything, even duping Zelo and Adasch.

With a final clicking of heels, First Sergeant Küttner looks up
from his journal: "The two supervisors from Barracks A, forward!"
Careful, there's something going on here, something we haven't seen
before. Every nerve in my body is alert. "You already know it . . . and
I can see that the two foremen are the guilty parties . . ." Why so
formal all of a sudden? If this were Lalka, I could understand, but
Kiewe? "As punishment, they will be sent to Camp 2 as common

laborers!" To the second camp—to the death camp. He'll be dead to us. It's over for him, for us, for our plan, for everything. "Off with the foreman armbands, camp elder. Take them off."

I am standing in the row just before the last one, among the taller men. So, now something has to happen. Yell, scream, attack, everyone—well, then roar and go charging out of the ranks, you first, out front. Well—well. Lalka, "the Doll," strides in and shouts into the commotion that has arisen: "Shut your traps! What kind of chaos is this?"

Küttner joins in: "Camp 1, attention! Everything that even resembles a man's shirt, off—down here, from left to right, by row." He is both pointing and threatening with his whip. His other hand is on his holster. "There are 734 men here. There will be 734 shirts or jackets on this pile. And I'll tell you, if I find a shirt on any one of you, you'll have to deal with me, and then it'll be the infirmary. Is that clear?"

I go directly to the sick bay, climb up on the bunk, and kneel down next to Robert. He is lying on his stomach, exuding a feverish stench, his face hidden between two skinny arms, his almost bald head shuddering in ceaseless sobs. The old Robert, the great theoretician, has shriveled into this heap.

In the barracks, up on the bunk, there is a gaping hole where Zelo's blanket roll used to be. I sense the stares coming my way from all sides. "It's already gotten around. Kiewe sent Zelo 'over there' simply because of a few filthy sports jackets. Schiffner, who as a Sudeten German thinks he understands our pals from Bohemia a little better, supposedly expressed the opinion that Zelo had just gotten to be too big for their liking—don't believe that they know anything, they'd have raised a lot bigger ruckus, but they suspect something. Maybe Kiewe, with all his experience as a jailer, knows that you can't allow groups to form and that you have to keep moving men around. If they knew anything for certain, it would've been off to the infirmary, and if they have cottoned on to something, then there has to be someone here who helped them . . ."

"Serves us right!" Hans is continuously shifting his body around in his bunk. "I mean us, here, not the Poles. We kept waiting, kept discussing. Shitheads, that's what we are, worse than the Poles here, because they've been that way all their lives—selling bad water, hustling and defrauding. But us, we arrived as if we had come from America or someplace like that. We knew, we understood, and we could've made heads roll. We're all of us man enough. But we've just pissed away all this time theorizing, bullshitting too long, getting everything ready, and in the meantime we've forgotten how to be human. We stood there like sheep today, not worth shit. They've already beat it all out of us."

Hans's cheeks are covered with red patches now. Over his pale complexion every single freckle is distinct. He surveys the entire room with a remote gaze. "My God, we're no longer human. I can't even believe in myself anymore, and all I can see is my old lady and my son over there on the other side—my little curly-headed son. When he was a tiny baby he had such delicate little cheeks, especially after his bath. We waved to each other when they separated us at the disrobing site. He stood there next to his mama and waved. You could see he was starting to get cold after leaving the train cars, where we had been warmed through. I was hoping that he wouldn't catch cold."

Hans paused. "The first day and night, after I had heard what happened to them, I didn't feel anything. It just didn't register. I just ran back and forth with those packs on my back, and I was only vaguely aware that they were 'over there.' Yeah, they're 'over there,' and I'm over here—that's all. It wasn't until a few more days had passed that, in the morning, my chest and my throat started to burn terribly, and my brain, as if some kind of acid had overflowed and spilled. And then suddenly in a craze, all I wanted was to tear down everything, like that long-haired man they told us about in religion class, who pulled down the pillars. You're crazy, I told myself. First you'll have to pull yourself together, collect your strength, clear your head. And that's what we all told ourselves—always too much thinking, not only here in Treblinka, but long before that, when it was all getting started with us. They wouldn't shut us up in ghettos like they used to in the old days, they wouldn't tear our heads off, and if they did, it might be one person, or two, but not all of us. They shut us all in. They will tear everyone's head off, in the end, even the Ukrainians who are their helpers. What good is reason here? What we need is one of those mad long-haired men who tore down the pillars and brought everything crashing to the ground."

Balkan Intermezzo

In our box we search for the last of the last rags to be processed. For hours we search through one and the same coat, turn it over, slide it around, pretend to be working. SS men pass by on their rounds, inattentive, lost in their own thoughts. There is nothing here. There is no reason to prod us on. We are slowly running out of work at Treblinka.

Little Abraham is approaching us from the box for women's coats. He is holding a crumpled photograph in his hand. "I found this in one of the last coats. In the arm, hidden in the cuff." Abraham hands the photo to David Brat, turning it over so that the back is facing David. David could be thirty-five, or he could just as well be forty, but the hands in which he is holding the wrinkled picture look as though they belong to an old man. His bloodless fingers are always contorted, and the joints are swollen.

"*Dla czego ja mam oddacz swoje mode zyczie w Treblince pod malkiniou.*" I hear David trying to make out the Polish words written on the back of the photo: "Why must I give up my young life here in Treblinka Malkinia?"

"David, David, that means that this young girl—that these people—knew. David, you all knew where your journey would end?"

"I told you before, we knew and we didn't know. After we saw who they were herding into the ghetto with us, we could guess. Back then, at the very beginning, a few of the young ones from Treblinka, and from some other places too, were able to escape. They went back to their ghettos and told everyone what was happening. Why did they go back there? When they must have known that they would be captured again and taken back to where there would be nothing but death?" David answers our next question before we ask: "Because they wanted to warn us, and because they knew there was no longer any place for them to hide. Nine of ten Poles, who hate all Germans, are so strongly anti-Semitic that they will turn in any Jew, especially if they get a reward for it. I heard of a case where a Pole in a small village had hidden a Jew, the Germans found out, and the Pole lit a fuse and blew himself to smithereens together with the Jew and everything in his house. These days, after three and a half years of war, you probably won't come across anymore Poles like that. And I know of other cases where they hid Jews: before midnight they separated him from his money, and after midnight they went to the German police to turn him in and collect the reward. I know that it is hard for you to imagine that something like this could be true. And you will probably find it hard to believe that we didn't believe the young men who fled back to the ghettos and told us their stories. Just imagine that you two, well no, not you, but two others, flee back to your people in Czechoslovakia and tell everything. You two would hear it, maybe not firsthand, but from someone else, who himself had heard it from someone or other. You wouldn't believe it either . . ."

David slowly takes a deep breath: "But now we have to find another way to let the world know and to prove that we don't belong in Treblinka, that no Jew belongs here—and every one of us here must take part . . . Yesterday we talked about this in the carpentry shop. Lublink was there, Simcha, people from the machine shop. Then Galewski and Dr. Choronzycki, too. We're going to start over again. Forget Plan H, because we don't know why they sent Zelo 'over there.' All of us here will have to . . . We know about the three informers, but otherwise every one of us here, every man, must do something . . ."

The next morning, under the rays of a sun that has not yet been able to drive the night cold from the work barracks, we hear an unfamiliar rhythmic clatter coming from the direction of the arrival ramp, and then suddenly it is interrupted by the squeal of brakes. These aren't the usual closed cars. On the flatbeds there are rails, and there are dumpers to be used in the construction of a narrow-gauge track. There are shovels and spades—everything brand-new, as if it had come directly from the factory. Even before the Blues and the Reds can unload this shipment, Miete and Bredow are making the rounds through Barracks A, looking for people box by box, and other SS men are doing the same thing in Barracks B. In no time they've assembled a new work commando of about sixty men. They keep herding more men onto the sorting site. The SS are energized. The whips start cracking again.

By noon a temporary rail siding has been laid across the entire sorting site, and the dumpers are rolling. Meanwhile word of the SS plan, put together for lack of real work to do, is already circulating through the camp. The entire sorting site, which is on a slight incline along the side leading away from the "infirmary"—as is the whole camp all the way to the headquarters building at the far end —is to be leveled.

Shortly after midday, having shed their long coats, Lalka, Kiewe, and a few others begin to arrive. Whenever the sun comes out from behind the clouds, the visors on the high caps glisten, and so do the boots.

From the entrance to the barracks, where dust-laden wedges of light pour in through the cracks, we observe the entire operation with the dumpers. Lalka is the first one to make a move. He gets hold of one of the men who has an awkward hand with a shovel, and right then and there, on the spot, he applies twenty-five lashes to his backside. Meanwhile Kiewe has also chosen a victim, and together with Sepp Hirtreiter he beats the exposed backside of the kneeling man. They are like smithies hammering away on an anvil with alternating blows. Then come strikes to the head and the face. The work tempo at the site picks up, in no time the dumpers are full, hauled off, their loads dumped, then back to the work site, back and forth, faster and faster—get moving, get moving—keep it going! "Concentration camp, a normal concentration camp, a forced labor camp, that's what it's supposed to look like here." Karl muses out loud as the SS depart the scene. "They've had enough for the time being, and now they're going to go down and get something to eat to restore their energy."

It's a moment to catch your breath and rest up against the wall. Faces are wiped. Then suddenly a fright runs through the herd again, as if they had spotted a raptor about to swoop down among them. The shovels have begun swinging. The foremen and Kapos are bellowing. Lalka, "the Doll," has appeared on the scene accompanied by his entourage.

At evening roll call you can clearly see who has been working with the dumpers. Reddened, anxious faces, clothes and boots gray from the dusty sand—this is an unfamiliar picture in Treblinka compared with the way it was before, when the entire work crew, with the exception of the men from the camouflage commando, appeared in surreptitiously polished boots and meticulously brushed jackets. It is a concentration camp, nothing but a common stinking KZ. And the way Lalka, after his coffee break, took a shovel to that man, is that part of the new order too?

Hans makes an entrance from the adjoining sorting barracks. They appointed him to replace Zelo as supervisor, just like that, because of his height and maybe because of his *Prager Dajtsch*, his Prague German, too. Angry, deep in his own thoughts, he lashes out with his own whip. One of his younger charges darts by, a small boy with a dumb expression. Hans turns brusquely in his direction and grabs him: "Come, come—come here—*tutej*—I said!" He pulls the boy close and glares down at him. My God, the kid's really afraid of him. "Where do you think you're going?"

"*Jach hab beim Chaver*—I left a piece of bread with my friend, in his pack," he smiles and answers in Yiddish.

"So, you're going out to get some fresh air, or something?" Hans nods somewhat benevolently, somewhat contemptuously. The boy repeats his answer in Polish. "Aha, you've got a piece of bread that you left with your friend, hmm. You asked him to keep it for you, hmm"—the boy nods in response—"and you're going to pick it up, hmm."

Hans pauses and then continues in his benevolent, contemptuous tone: "Well, first, you don't have anymore bread, because you stuffed it down your throat the moment you got your paws on it. Now wait, don't interrupt, let me finish, devoured it the moment you got it, the same way I do." Keeping count, Hans extends an index finger next to an extended thumb: "Second, you wouldn't give your bread to your dear little pal, even if they threatened to cut your balls off, because you know he would cram it down his own little throat. And third, but this doesn't even really come into play"—Hans has started a biting conversation with himself, and the kid looks up at him, puzzled or maybe understanding all too well—"if you were really dumb enough to give it to him, then he's already gobbled it up. And now

I'll tell you where you're going. You're running off to do some deal, something with your *Chaver*, some speculation with your little pal— *zkrencic papirosu*—roll a cigarette or two." Hans mimes the production of a cigarette, and then he lets loose: "And you can't tell me the truth? You have to try to dupe me too? Am I one of those—like Kapo Fritz in Barracks B over here, where he gets his share of every little piece of crap they speculate, even when you're getting it in your ugly little mug? Now get to work! If there's any work you can do!"

"Honzo, Honzo—Hans, calm down!" Karl reprimands him. Hans gives the kid a shove and sends him running.

David approaches him, and I can barely hear what he is whispering: "If you are born sometime during or after a pogrom, if everything is burning and crashing down around your mama, then maybe you will be like him. And you won't know yourself whether you're telling the truth or a lie. And from then on you'll be carrying around a Jewish *Mojre*—a fear." David's bright blue eyes open wider, and his front teeth are showing again: "This Jewish *Mojre*—that's what we have to escape."

For a while there is silence. "Over there, they're doing something with the dumpers. But they're not just loading and unloading sand."

"Now they've started digging up the bodies from the first transports."

"Well, they'll have to put all the pieces in their hats. They're falling apart."

"And they're burning them." David takes a deep breath through his nose. "Can't you tell by the smell?"

The clothing boxes have all been emptied. They take us, the remaining fifteen men from Barracks A, over to a large heap of cinders at the far end of the platform, right next to the entrance gate. We are to carry cinders to Barracks A, spread them over the floor in each box, and over the aisles too, and then tamp them down into a smooth surface. The Reds and the Blues are taking cinders from the same heap and using them to resurface the grounds of the train station.

The SS are beginning to lose interest. They hardly notice the men filling the dumpers. The shovels have stopped swinging at such a breakneck tempo. Laboring figures are beginning to wilt, resting on shovel handles. From time to time they push a full dumper down the tracks; then it rolls slowly back, the men pushing it step by step.

In two boxes in Barracks A, where we could easily finish off the floors in an hour and a half, we're loafing around for the second day.

"*Achtung*" comes ringing in from the entrance, and there's Lalka marching into the barracks. Not even the usual "Carry on" passes his lips. All he does is have those grotesque figures stand at attention, their eyes agape from hunger and weakness. He stops not far from us, surveys the empty boxes with a scrutinizing eye, inspects us briefly, then turns aside full of officiousness and solemnity, and broadcasts into the emptiness of the barracks: "Beginning tomorrow, transports will again be arriving, and it will be back to work for you." He nods to himself and disappears through the opening of the doorway.

"Hans, Foreman Hans!" a voice bellows out of the adjacent sorting barracks. Hans flies out and then races back in, dropping his whip along the way and picking it back up. He doesn't come to a final stop until he almost falls over the workbench we have just moved back onto the dampened and tamped cinder floor of our box. "No more transports from Poland. They're coming from abroad now. Kiewe just told me. I'm supposed to have everything perfectly set up. For tomorrow they've scheduled big transports from abroad." Almost no one lifts a finger for the rest of the day. At the sorting site the SS are just hanging around, quietly talking in twos or in small groups, as if they didn't even notice the intense discussions going on around the dumpers. The entire camp is overcome with feverish anticipation.

The excitement over the new transports reaches a crescendo that evening in our sleeping quarters. "Well, I'd really like to know where . . . Theresienstadt . . . most likely. Do you have any relatives still living there? Of course, you weren't there for that long, but me, I know everybody I lay my eyes on back there. If I can manage it, I'll run up to Suchomel and tell him to bring that guy out. He's my brother."

"Aha, you'll be doing him a special *Meziehe*, a favor, especially if he's got his wife and child with him. And what if you see fifteen or twenty people you know?"

"Couldn't we finally do something if a transport like that arrives?"

"We haven't done a thing before, and now you want to start something? Now, when we're all as hungry as stray dogs? Just take a look at how many whips there are. I would like to be able to see deep inside"—Robert is pointing to his own chest—"and know if they're thinking about the others who will be arriving after them, or about all the feed they'll be bringing."

"And you, how do you know so much?" Hans asks, more subdued than not. "Who did you get it from, who said . . . ?"

At morning roll call we are given strict orders not to leave our workplaces in the barracks. They've even chased the men off the sorting site and spread them out among the work barracks. About an hour later the first cars roll up to the platform.

This time, standing in my empty box, I can observe the arrival ramp through a crack between the boards. Freight cars—cattle cars—so it is a Polish or a Russian transport after all. People climb calmly out of the cars, without pushing, without crowding. It is easy to see that they've come a long way. Apparently they have been in quarantine too. Their clothes are wrinkled and dirty, but they are good clothes, items of value. Their faces look healthy, and they have an unusually dark complexion. Black hair—all I see is black to pitch-black hair. On the left side, mostly on the left coat collar, each of them has a small yellow star. This is the first time I've seen stars like this—I'll have to wait until a few of them pass by. The star is very small, framed in black, without any lettering. And now I can see that they've been pinned on like brooches. Not made of fabric, but of some kind of material, maybe wood. I can hear that the people are speaking a completely foreign language.

"Let me see!" David Brat pushes his way in, presses his face up against the boards, and tries to catch the attention of one of the passing Blues, but his voice is lost in the activity on the platform: "Moniek, can you hear me, Moniek! Mietek! Hey, Kuba, where are they from?"

"Bulgaria, the Balkans" is the answer we hear through the wooden wall.

In the frozen silence—no one notices how long it lasts—we again hear the first words from David: "Look, they're already running, undressed." He's pointing toward the sorting site.

Kiewe's deep green uniform stands out from the crowd of naked bodies. He's running out in front of them, bellowing something, something that sounds like "heya-heya." He keeps turning around, checking, and accompanied by other SS and guards, he leads the entire retinue of naked bodies down to the presorting barracks across from ours. He shows them where to put their clothes, their coats, their underwear—everything in separate piles. Then, in double time, he leads them back, and the naked bodies reappear, this time with shoes in hand, running in the direction of the Barracks for Notions and Sundries, Barracks B.

I hadn't expected there would be anything like this under those wrinkled clothes. Brown, muscular bodies shivering slightly in the coolness of a dark, cloudy day. Thick hair, broad shoulders, well-formed bodies. A young, handsome man with dark skin runs by, his black mane of hair streaming, with a profile that might have been carved. Two youths approach each other; they can't be more than eighteen years old. Behind them is a man whose beard is just turning gray, a proud figure with a full chest, thigh muscles taut under the skin. I've seen these three somewhere before: these three, the old one, it's Laocoön and his sons. From my schoolbooks and the pictures in the hallway, I knew them. And more follow.

"Look," Karl yells, amazed. "There's nothing left on the sorting site. They had to carry everything to the barracks themselves. They've done the presort themselves. Not a single blow, everything without whips. They have no idea." With a nod of his head he points in the direction of an SS man. "They've planned this and prepared. That's why we had to stay in the barracks."

The dumpers are standing on the sorting site, deserted and covered in dust. The last one is still tipped over a small pile of sand. No one righted the box once the news of the transport had spread. These dumpers, by chance, are playing an unusual role. They have a calming effect on these handsome naked people, silently telling them, "Don't worry, just look at us. Look, there's work to be done. This is just an ordinary work camp. You'll be put to work here."

At the corner below the rampart, the last of the naked bodies disappears beyond the side entrance to the disrobing site, from where they had carried off their clothing, and the green wall closes behind them. "And now, shivering through the Pipeline directly into the baths," Hans accompanies them with his remarks. "Bulgaria, Greece —if it keeps up like this, pretty soon they'll be hauling them in from Palestine . . ."

"Everybody out, out onto the platform, unload these cars!" Kiewe appears at the door, drooling from the corners of his mouth. Together with the others, I run out of the barracks. Along the way we meet up with some men who are already carrying luggage, even a few who are surreptitiously chewing behind closed mouths. Yeah, their mouths are full, and their faces are completely transformed, brightened.

As I come through the main gate I am suddenly overcome with an enormous, dazzling spectacle. The dream, the passionate, inescapable dream of an incessantly hungry man here in Treblinka is unfolding before me on the arrival ramp. But no, no—not one of us could have imagined it, not in his hungriest fantasies: only about half of the cars had carried passengers; the other half was packed full of boxes, chests, sacks, huge balls sewn together from blankets. The Blues are carrying cases full of marmalade down to the supply depot. Someone bumps into them, and a box breaks open—it had been helped along—and they fall down, delighted and overjoyed, into the sticky, dark red morass. They get up slowly, mouths full. They swallow, and the whips are cracking over their heads until the dark red goo is enriched with the blood from their faces.

Meat—huge pieces of dried, pale-colored meat are lying on the platform, falling out of the cars along with any number of packs so full that they burst open upon hitting the ground. The black cinder surface is covered with countless small yellow cookies that are crushed underfoot as the men go back and forth to the platform. Like a pale yellow streusel they cover the nearby luggage, the leather suitcases, the pots of marmalade, the scattered pillows with their intricate needlepoint. I return for the second time and immediately cram my mouth full of the thick little golden squares—a wonder, an unimaginable delight at the first swallow. Your face relaxes. Now, now I must have that same strange look as the ones who were the first to come back from the platform.

At the sight of this flood of food and goods spread out in front of a herd of men enfeebled by hunger, the first part of Treblinka is gripped by feverish activity. And the second part, the death camp? The men over there won't get anything but these naked bodies, and it's just these muscular types that are supposed to be so difficult to burn.

Fifteen, twenty minutes was all it lasted, the entire action. We're already back in our boxes. The empty cars are slowly pulling out.

Again the scream of a whistle, and another lot pulls in. Little Abraham comes dashing in from the platform, drops what he's carrying, raises his arms high into the air, and reports, groaning in amazement: "Cheese again, tons of cheese, big as mill wheels . . ." During the midday break, the soup bowls are stacked up half full by the trees in front of the mess and all along the barracks wall. A few tip over, puddles form, and a large potful of thin gruel is being carried out— and dumped into the latrine.

In the afternoon, by the time other sections of the transport have arrived, we have managed to partly fill our box with coats. Where is Sergeant Schiffner with the cigarettes he wants to trade for an elegant coat? The pockets of all of these coats are filled with all different kinds of cigarettes. "*Nie czloweku*—no, man, I only smoke the best cigarettes now, first class." The little foreman from the presorting barracks, with his duck face and raspy voice, indicates to one of his people that he's only interested in the cigarette packs with the roman numeral one on the front—first class—*pierszi Gatuniek.*

"Okay, okay, okay, for us, from now on, nothing but first class— *pierszi Gatuniek.* Anyway, we're all *pierszi Gatuniek,* first class. After all, hadn't they chosen us from among all of the Jews and prepared us to become the best of our line?" Who knows if our little colleague foreman understands the Bohemian musings of Hans Freund?

We are sent up to the presorting barracks to get things in order, to make room. Speculation is rife. "If you come across anything especially good to drink, and cigarettes, put them aside for me somewhere, okay? Maybe some women's lingerie, and you can make up a little package for Zelo too. Food, underwear, shoe polish—I'll take it to him. He sends his greetings." The casually elegant, still slim Master Sergeant Karl Ludwig, a bright sort in his middle years, no more spent than average, has come out of the death camp on a brief foray to our *Kirmes,* our Christmas market, to get a share of the riches as long there are still riches to be had. In return, he has brought our first, and totally unexpected, news of Zelo, for whom he will even be doing a small favor.

Bredow mentions in passing that he's interested in a suitcase of the very best leather, and maybe a little cologne or perfume. "Apart from that, you can do what you want," Bredow, as head of the work site, lets it be known, "just make sure you keep an eye out for the first sergeant." He means Küttner-Kiewe.

"And watch out for Master Sergeant Franz, too," Gentz and Seidel add to the same refrain, more for their own benefit than for ours. They're looking for shaving supplies.

Yessir, sergeant sir, boss sir, how well we've come to understand one another. It's only Lalka, Kiewe, Miete the knucklehead, and two or three idiots like Boelitz who really eat this assignment up—and Stangl of course, the commandant of the entire camp. Only they would get us for speculation and really go for the jugular. But the ones who do not, or no longer go by the book, will do what they can to protect us.

Three were chosen from this transport. We observe them from a distance, inconspicuously. By twilight, exhausted and leaning up against the pine trees in front of the mess, they slurp hot ersatz coffee from tin cups. One of us remarks in passing: "They weren't saved for work. They'd be good in a museum. Now I guess they're gonna set up a museum here in Treblinka." All three of them are older. Two are teachers, and one is a rabbi. They were the transport leaders. They can speak a little, a very little German. Through them the others were informed that everything had to be disinfected, that they would go to a bath to be disinfected, and then they would be sent to work. You can tell by the way the three of them are standing there that, for the time being, they have been left to believe that this is true. As for what they thought they smelled amid all the commotion, they believed it was lime or some other disinfectant. And they still know nothing more.

Even when Karl speaks German, in his natural, east Moravian way, people respond to him as openly as they would to a neighbor: "Where are you from? Are there any ghettos where you come from?"

The man who has been asked these questions shakes his head: "No, we don't have any ghettos. We come—came—from a detention camp in Salonika."

"Did you know where you would be going?"

"They told us we would be going to Poland to a newly built ghetto to join others of our kind . . . We spent about a half a year in the camp in Salonika. They brought in Jews from Bulgaria, Greece, Yugoslavia . . . There were about twenty-four thousand of us there . . . That—in our most horrible dreams . . ."

"And what was it like in the camp in Salonika?"

"Not so bad. We could buy what we needed. We owned many things in common. We lived as a community, sharing everything we needed." We could tell that by what they brought, and how they brought it. We don't ask any more questions. It looks as if they have turned their remote gaze entirely inward.

From somewhere near the green barbed-wire fence, the drunken bawl of a Ukrainian guard, masked by darkness, gives way to an abundant melody: "*w podweczer my hulali, Natascha cilowala mene* —by twilight we strolled, Natasha kissed me again and again . . ."

Tonight the sound of the barracks is completely different from last night. Exuberant screams. Laughter, satisfied expressions everywhere. People are stuffed, hot, and glistening with sweat and fat. Over there someone is shoveling out plum butter with one cookie after another. Nearby, a hand can be seen holding a piece of cornbread piled high with cheese. Beyond two rows of bunks, in a sudden flare of candlelight, I catch sight of a shiny, oval tin of fish falling out of someone's unzipped pants.

"Good God, can't you stop stuffing your faces!" Hans stands up shouting and leans in the direction of the opposite bunk. The two he's looking at are the same ones I haven't been able to ignore for the last little while. They've been wolfing down *Mamaliga*—roasted corn kernels coated with sugar—incessantly.

"*Co tie to obchodi, Chonsa*—Hans, what does it matter to you?" is the response, in Polish, from the other bunk.

"It does matter to me, a lot. I can't stand the sight of you, the way you've been stuffing your faces for the past hour."

"Well, let's remember we're in Treblinka," the usual platitude.

"Jesus Christ, do you have to behave like animals!" Red patches have started to appear on Hans' cheeks.

"Jesus Christ . . ." someone is mimicking Hans, "what kind of a Jew have we got here? How did he ever get to Treblinka?"

Others chime in: "Right, something better—a cultured Czech— and does exactly what we do, but with intelligence."

Before we can stop him, Hans is hanging across the passageway between the bunks, holding himself on a post with one hand, cracking his whip into the emptiness with the other: "You pack—filthy Poles! I hate you, if you have to know, just like I hate them. I hate you for all your deceit and trickery . . ." We pull Hans back to his bunk so that he's only bellowing at us: "Franz was right: wallowing in their own shit, just wallowing in their own shit . . ."

"Jew anti-Semite—German dupe!" The opposite bunk has the last word.

Robert hands the half-sitting, half-lying Hans a thermometer, pulls down his lower eyelids and examines the whites of his eyes. "Yes, yes, 'Treblinka' has caught up with him! And it seems to be developing unusually fast, somehow . . ."

For four days the cars pull in fully loaded and pull out empty. Women and children go away and disappear into the barracks on the disrobing site. The handsome brown-complected male bodies trot across the sorting site past the deserted dumpers and then trot away into eternity—Bulgarians, Greeks, Yugoslavs.

These days all we do is cover the thirty meters, with Karl, between our box and the presort barracks. Because the clothing is still warm from body heat, it has gotten very stuffy in here again. Our own bodies are overheated from the oil in the canned fish, strong alcohol, and the like.

Bredow, Schiffner, Seidel, and a few others have already got more than one suitcase, all full, all whisked down to their barracks. Gentz, always the rascal, somewhat bewildered and blithe, selected his two leather bags right at the platform upon the arrival of one part of the transport. But at the moment he was about to casually take one into his own hands, Küttner-Kiewe appeared on the scene. The quick-witted Gentz immediately shoved the suitcase at one of the Blues, and with blows raining down from his whip, he herded the man around to the other side of the barracks. He more or less feigned the blows, and the Blue seemed to understand what was happening. "Ow, owowow, ow, sir, please sir . . ." Gentz kept it up until Kiewe left. Then he directed one of the boys to carry the two bags off to an empty box, where he emptied the contents, kept the cognac and the cigarettes, and left the rest behind. He then made his way to the box for women's lingerie, where he filled one of the suitcases again.

By the fifth day it seemed as if everything had been switched off: no whistle, no transports. Through the doorway of Barracks A I can see one lonely figure standing on top of the rampart—Captain Stangl wearing a white uniform jacket. A riding crop swings gently from the hand he is holding behind his back. He's looking down into the other camp. There he can see a bright plume of smoke rising and then disintegrating into the cool freshness of the early morning.

Later, by the time the sun has reached its zenith, a steamy sweet stench has thickened the late March air.

All of the barracks and presorting rooms are full up to the ceilings. Kiewe has started raging and applying pressure again. His furious wrath affects the others. Within two weeks everything has been sorted, bundled, and packed. Empty cars arrive, and even more pressure is applied. A long chain of bodies carrying bundles is ceaselessly running between the ramp and the work sites. New cars keep arriving empty and then pulling out fully loaded. One day we are again standing in the silence of the barracks with its empty boxes, rummaging around in the few remaining rags, from time to time looking out at the work site, where the dumpers have been put back into operation. Willy and Salo, both from the Gold Jew commando, are making their usual rounds with their little cases. Even though the currencies have no value here, they take the last of the Bulgarian leva, Serbian dinars, and Greek drachmas from the boxes that hang on the wall posts. The louis d'or that arrived with the transports have disappeared, and are disappearing, along the same routes as did the gold dollars and the rubles.

Little Willy Fürst, a hotelier from Moravian Ostrów, is probably the best informed of those of us from Theresienstadt. He spends most of his time sitting down at the big depository, where he can easily observe the comings and the goings of the SS. Through a window he can watch the traffic in front of the SS barracks in the direction of the headquarters building. He hears a lot on the inside, because some of them are always hanging around, especially the higher-ups. Among the twelve members of the Gold Jew commando, Willy always seems to be playing some kind of a supporting role: slightly ironic and always alert, absurdly serious and cynical, and aloof, he is like a bank officer who has only been sent here from somewhere else to help out. Even some of us get confused about the number of keys in which Willy is playing at any one time. The black eyes, bushy eyebrows, the mustache under his nose, his somewhat rotund figure—they all add to the confusion. Franz likes this, while Küttner has no appreciation of such nuances. The younger and more handsome Salo Sauer is often quite morose and uncommunicative. Otherwise it would be impossible for them to form the kind of partnership they have. They are twins in a different way from the way that Karl and I are twins, but similar in that they share blankets, spoons, and thoughts.

We learn from Willy that the masters are unusually happy with their take from the Balkan transports. None of the previous transports had brought in such a generous amount of supplies. There was less money and fewer valuables, however. That's where the Polish transports take the lead, even if they are full of lice. "They really have got us well trained. In the past we never seemed to be able to get control of the mountains of things. Now, in less than three weeks, it looks as though those twenty-four thousand people had never even come through here. And now we're adding to the riches in the big depository. Next week they'll probably be withdrawing some of the money and the gold and transferring it to Lublin. But don't worry," Willy changes tone, "they're not going to take everything. They'll leave enough here to meet their everyday needs. After all, we have an understanding."

"Do you people down there have any idea how much money has already passed through your hands?"

"How should we know? Impossible. Do you think we give them accurate numbers? Let's assume that after all the speculation and chicanery that goes on, about a third of the money ends up in the depository. And then we, the higher-ups and us, speculate with that. We also hide and bury money, gold, and jewelry, just like you do up there. There are twelve of us in the commando, and we all speculate. We all have people in our living quarters who bring us food. And the SS boys do business with us in the depository the same way they do business with you up there. Not a one of them, not Suchomel, not even his bosses, is interested in all that much order and precision. If this ever got to headquarters in Lublin, or better yet, in Berlin! Not long ago Küttner and Franz almost got into a real fight. I could see them through the window standing across from each other. Küttner was bursting with rage, screaming about how all this was a big, ugly mess, and he was going to tell Berlin what was happening here. You see, Franz is thought to be speculating too, but no one knows exactly what he's doing. Actually, now that we've got a few things moving again, I wouldn't want the top to know too much about the money business down here. They'd transfer us, and reassign the SS boys. We'd get some new ones, greedy and not yet full enough . . ."

Willy changes his tone again and says as he leaves: "You'll have to build it up within your own organization. The way the commandos work with the Kapos and the foremen. We have to pay very careful attention to the leaky points." Followed by Salo, Willy heads off down the passageway between the stalls, swinging his little case and shouting like a carnival barker: "Money, gold, precious stones, jewelry of all kinds . . ."

The Uniformed Riders of the Antichrist

We have started going to the inconspicuous evening meetings down at the workshops again. First of all, we have to be certain that there are a few trustworthy people in each of the commandos, then we'll work with them individually and organize the entire group into a fighting unit. Kapo Rakowski will have to be given a special assignment, especially now that Camp Elder Galewski is lying in sick bay with what appears to be a rather severe case of "Treblinka."

We all know that Rakowski is a loner here at Treblinka, but he is a powerful one who doesn't need anyone else. He's not close to anyone; no one can ever be certain if Rakowski means what he says and does. He is the biggest speculator in the entire camp, a glutton, a boozer, a bellyacher. And he's not looking out for anyone but himself; everything he does is for his own benefit. If they ever catch him, he won't have anymore friends. But they don't want to catch him. If they had wanted to get him, they could've done it a long time ago. Up until now, it's seemed to have suited their purposes just to let him be. The guards admire him because he's such a giant and can bellow like a bull. Supposedly they will get him anything he wants. They're always doing deals with him. And he's always got a piece of ham, a little bottle of vodka, and a handful of banknotes stuffed into oversized jodhpurs that look as if they've been inflated. His lackeys must have had to search a while before they found a pair of pants large enough to contain his enormous behind and his two beefy thighs. There's one additional distinguishing characteristic: those beefy thighs merge downward into a pair of skinny knock-kneed legs.

But if Rakowski is on such good terms with the guards, couldn't he find out how they would respond in certain situations? Couldn't he let them know that the *Germancy*—the Germans—are about to lose this war? With the help of their guards, some of the commandos, who had been on the outside gathering construction materials, had even managed to smuggle in a few newspapers. There are some encouraging things to be read between the lines. And a few of the SS have started wandering around deep in thought, mumbling to themselves: "Shit, all of it shit!"

If Rakowski really does know how to get whatever he wants out of the guards, how about a pistol, or any kind of weapon, in return for a pile of money, gold, and jewelry, of course? That kind of thing can easily be buried, and then if you've got money, lots of money, you can overcome all sorts of adversity, no matter how things develop. Actually, it's time for Rakowski to show what he can do, now that they've named him to replace Camp Elder Galewski.

But how are we going to get to Rakowski? Who can get that close? But wait, there is someone Rakowski listens to—Cescha, our robust peasant woman, as Hans puts it. She works in the German mess, and the few girls who are here look up to her the same way we looked up to Zelo.

And now that we cannot be certain what will happen with Galewski, Dr. Choronzycki—Chorazycki is how it's really spelled in Polish—is also emerging as one of the leaders in our common endeavor. He was taken off a Polish transport so that he could work in the German dentist's office. We don't see much of Choronzycki. He pretty much limits his activities to the area around the ghetto and his workplace, which is across the way from the big depository. His face is pale, and his posture makes him look old, expressionless, insignificant. It is better and less risky to keep having him get money from the depository, rather than depending on the Gold Jews themselves.

These days the noonday sun is quite warm. As we approach the mess for our midday break, we notice that four guards are carrying some kind of bloody bundle away from the SS barracks. The bundle is being carried by the hands and feet, the only sign that this is something human.

"Dr. Choronzycki" is the name passed among the crowd. Before we can make our way up to the tin bowls and empty them while standing around in our groups in subdued confusion, we learn what happened. This morning Lalka dropped into the German sick bay and wanted to get some kind of medication from Choronzycki, who was there alone. Suddenly, on impulse, Lalka wanted to know what Choronzycki had in his big bag. He found 150,000 zloty, along with lots of dollars, everything loose, probably stuffed into the bag on the fly. Choronzycki jumped Franz. But Franz, both younger and bigger, quickly got the upper hand. Choronzycki was still able to escape and run out of the office, but that's when the SS came rushing up and beat him to the ground. A special roll call will be held before we return to afternoon work. There are more SS than usual, more alert, and Lalka is going to speak, already having dusted himself off and groomed for the occasion.

"There," he points with his whip at the bloody bundle on the ground in front of him. Coated with cinders, the body is lost in shredded clothing. "There, you can see what happens when you're crazy enough to attack one of us." Lalka takes a few steps forward, his eyes wide open, taking in the rows and each man in them. "I want to know where he got all of that money! He spent all of his time working down at the dentist's office. He couldn't have got it on his own. I want to know how he got it . . ."

Two of the guards pour two buckets of water over the bundle, and when the body stirs ever so slightly, others appear carrying a wooden stand. This is Lalka's newest acquisition. He had it made in the carpentry shop so that he could mete out his punishments on the assembly site for the benefit of his entire public—twenty-five, fifty blows on the clothed backside, on the naked backside . . . They lay the shriveled heap over the stand. From the front they have to hold it by the hands because it keeps falling back under the force of Lalka's blows. Suddenly, after about the fifteenth lash, the body shudders, collapses, and no longer moves. The next blows land dully, as if on a half-filled sack—thirty, thirty-one . . . Franz is no longer striking with such care and deftness; the whip is no longer cracking rhythmically so high over his head. The sack hanging over the stand simply absorbs the blows rather than reacting to them. Forty-eight, forty-nine, fifty—Lalka has lost his balance a few times and stumbled forward. "Now, to the infirmary to be shot!"

So this little scene was no real success. He escaped you before the curtain fell, and you had to play it out alone without an opposite. We've all been in Treblinka long enough to know, even from a dis-

tance, when a man is finished. Lalka straightens his jacket. The tails
had pulled out over his belt. "The Jew swine—the *Saujud*—had to
have money . . . I know, the Gold Jews—I want the Gold Jews—get
them up here—one at a time!"

As evening approaches, the call resounds through Barracks A:
"Money, gold, jewelry—turn over everything—to the trusted Gold
Jews!"

After the inquest Willy leaps over the wooden stand: "That's what
happened down there, but up here we got the worst of it. Everyone
stripped, and one after the other we were marched right up to the
infirmary pit. He grilled each one of us, holding his pistol to our
backs. He kept asking who had given money to Choronzycki, why,
and who was still hiding money . . ."

"Suddenly it began to look," Salo joined in, "as if we had nothing
but the infirmary to look forward to. It also looked as though the
rest of the SS boys were keeping their distance, leaving the Doll his
solo appearance, and the sole responsibility, in Stangl's eyes, for the
annihilation of every special commando unit in Treblinka. Otherwise, how can anyone explain why we were released again?"

"He did well—Choronzycki. It's not really clear whether they
killed him or not. Word's going around that he managed to gulp
something down. In any case, it looks as if there's still work to be
done here, even if we don't get any more transports. They want to
keep the camp; if not, you wouldn't find a camp like Treblinka so far
behind the front."

It's almost a miracle. Hans walked out of the sick bay on his own
two legs. They've gotten very thin and spindly, to be sure, and they
rattle around in what are now oversized boots, but we'll take care of
that. At roll call and marches, we'll help hold him up from the back
and both sides, we'll look out for him in the work barracks, and
whenever danger nears, we'll quickly raise him up from the pile of
rags where he's half sitting and half lying.

Galewski is also on his feet again, but he is still so unsteady that
Rakowski is to continue as camp elder until Galewski gets his
strength back. Whenever there is more work in camp besides the
transports, whenever things are being remodeled, rebuilt, or expand-
ed, the SS turn a blind eye to those who are merely "cleaning up
their own shit"—especially when it comes to the camp elder. Other-

wise they root through everything in sight. And they've even taken people away from the workshops and assigned them to the dumpers. New commando units have been formed, and they leave the camp, under guard, to load gravel, cinder, and other building materials. By the time the next transport arrives Treblinka will look like a park; Lalka is supposed to have made this pronouncement recently.

The sorting site, which had previously been one huge swarming mound, is now one of the quietest places in camp. Having been "retrained," one of the commando units from the sorting site is now known as the Woodcutters. They clear out the underbrush and cut down trees around the perimeter of the camp where the forest has become too dense.

Several of the commando units have been working outside the camp. Once you go a little deeper into the woods, the speculators start showing up, one by one, but these people are at the very bottom of the speculation chain. Barefoot boys and girls, raggedy beings, appear and then immediately disappear into the distance among the trees. They look as if they are there to collect dry branches. But actually, no more than a few steps away, they have hidden a packet.

The guards still have their pockets full of money, but they lure even more valuables out of the hungry men in the commando units—mostly dollars and gold. They skillfully discern who among the SS is a *dobry chef*—"a good boss," with whom they can do a deal, and they also learn with whom they cannot.

Then suddenly the guards disperse, except for one, who hangs back in the woods and quickly catches up again. Behind his back he's carrying a large bundle wrapped in brownish paper. A little farther on, he stops in a hollow, opens the packet, and invites the SS and the guards to help themselves. Sausages, hams, loaves of bread, small bottles of vodka—it looks as if by chance the guard has come across some kind of special bonus here in the area. Now they herd the entire commando unit together and leave it somewhere off to the side. Then each of them selects whatever he likes. And finally, the guard, again at the appropriate moment, lets a thing or two drop near the commando unit, in return for the twenty-dollar bill that was left near a tree stump. But the guard had not used this money to make his purchase. He has simply added it to the other valuables he already has hidden outside of Treblinka. He paid for his purchases with Polish zloty he has stuffed into his jodhpurs and covered up with the long shirt of his uniform. The SS pretend not to notice. No one sees anything, no one knows anything. After a short time there is not even the slightest sign. Everything proceeds with quiet consensus.

The performance continues as the work crew returns to camp. "If I catch anyone taking anything into camp," the SS man shouts threateningly, but somewhat more in the direction of the guards. Meanwhile he is having one of the guards carry in a smallish packet for him, and he takes care to see that he gets it back to his room unobserved. Everyone is smuggling food and drink into camp. The Ukrainians simply carry their booty behind their backs; all they have to worry about is a few whiplashes—twenty-five or fifty administered at roll call somewhere behind their barracks. The brave speculators in the work crew are carrying sausage, ham, and white bread somewhere against their naked skin—in their pants legs, under their shirts, in their armpits—and will keep it there until they get back to their living quarters that evening. There they will sell small pieces for twenty or thirty dollars, or for a thousand or fifteen hundred zloty, in order to have hard currency for their next excursion outside the camp. And this small piece of white bread, or this orange to be shared, will benefit the next man who finds himself lying in the sick bay. Without these bits of contraband, survival in Treblinka might well have been impossible.

My God, how have they been able to find so much food in this fourth year of the war in this miserable, wasted land? Where barefoot people in rags sell delicacies for twenty thousand zloty and gold watches . . . ? The answers we hear from David Brat and the others who come from the area around Warsaw all end the same way: "You can't really understand unless you have lived here in Poland for some time, especially here in the eastern part of the country. In the so-called Generalgouvernement, as the Germans have officially been referring to these areas since the Polish campaign, you will not get so much as one stamp on your ration card for bread. But on the black market, for outrageous sums of money, you can get whatever you want."

Everybody's speculating. The price gouging starts with the farmers, and the others keep pushing it further, and the biggest speculators and blackmailers of all are the Germans and their helpers. From somewhere beyond the Vistula, or maybe ever further west, you can follow the path of destruction the Germans have left behind them as they advanced eastward through the forests and across endless plains with their burned-out villages and hamlets. They are no more interested in genuine order than the SS are here in Treblinka—when it comes to matters of money, gold, and jewelry. Of course, we're not talking about the very top. It's the ones under them, the smaller ones and the little ones, and all of these goods will in some way run through their hands. If you were to start out on a journey through these regions, you would soon see that the same piece of bread that cost you twenty zloty somewhere in central Poland would cost twice as much east of Warsaw, and that the closer you came to Treblinka, the more expensive it would become; and inside Treblinka itself, you would have to pay five hundred zloty—or ten dollars, or five gold rubles—for three hundred grams of bread.

On this journey you would see the rage of the German SS, the provincial police, and the Polish Germans, known here as *Volksdeutsche*. A few kilometers farther into the woods you would come upon the partisans, and then a gang with nothing more in common with partisans than the name. They rob, and they murder; they don't care whom they attack by night. The entire region is in chaos, and at the center of it all, hidden behind its sandy ramparts, among forests at a bend in the Bug River, is Treblinka. It draws speculators from as far as one hundred kilometers away. But the vagabonds who make their timid appearance here among the trees, to be discovered by an eager guard, are only the last link in the chain. The big speculators are sitting at home in Warsaw and Lublin, where there are even supposed to be special organizations who send their people with truckloads of goods out to the huts around Treblinka. The entire region, far and near, sucks blood out of this greedy slaughterhouse. It is in their direct interest to keep Treblinka going, to keep its valuable byproducts flowing—money, gold, diamonds.

"If through some miracle you should ever be able to get out, then you can never let anyone know that you are fleeing Treblinka," Lublink tells us. "They would tear your clothes off your body, piece by piece, they'd kill you, and then they'd probably search you to see if you had any money on you . . ."

"Today we're going on a drive," Bredow announces, taking charge of our unit directly after morning roll call. He leads us past headquarters to a truck where ten Blues are already waiting with Sergeant Schiffner and a few guards. After we pass through the main entrance a sentry raises the control gate. At first the raw cold of the forest and the clouds, hanging over the deep black crowns of the motionless pines, have such a powerful impact on me that I don't even notice where we are going. Following a broad arc, we are again approaching the railroad tracks. We come to a clearing. Here, at the edge of the forest, the truck makes a sharp turn onto a road. I look back. Looking east, along the edge of the forest, I see that the road and the railway run parallel. Next to a large sign reading "Treblinka Labor Camp," the single-track siding and the transition from highway to forest road are barely noticeable. On one side of the highway there is a small station house labeled in more modest lettering "Treblinka," and along the other side of the road, stretching into the distance, there are swampy patches of land covered with tangled brush. Water is glistening in deep, sunken tracks left behind by cattle, and in places you can see black chunks of cut peat.

Out in front of us, where the dust is swirling over the road, we can see the first shelter, a hut weighted down with bundles of straw that look like shaggy pelts. "The railway continues on past the hut in the direction of Białystok to the east, and in the opposite direction to Malkinia," one of the Blues explains. "It looks as if we'll be going to the sawmill to pick up some lumber. Not long ago one of the units delivered a load of logs. Look, we're going to go through a small village now. It's called Kotaski. The people all look as if they're about to die, and they live in miserable huts, but I'll bet that, hidden away somewhere, they've got a little sack of money and gold from Treblinka."

"These people, here?" another Blue chimes in. "How can that be? All they're left with is crumbs. They have to turn over just about everything they've got to the speculators who distribute the goods, and even they have to turn over whatever they get . . ."

"*A jak nie*—and if they don't, if they don't turn it over?"

"Then they'll have the partisans on their tails. Or they'll get fingered as partisans themselves and reported to the Germans."

And now we're driving past some of the thatched huts. Out in front there are children, teenagers, and women, all of them barefoot and dressed in rags, all of them standing there with their mouths wide open, some trying to cover their mouths with their hands. They all gape at the trucks racing past, following the progress of this terrifying apparition—the uniformed riders of the Antichrist from the realm of the dead, of gold and legendary riches, beyond the forest. For a little bottle of vodka, or a little bottle of cream, you can get boots made of leather so soft that you wear them like gloves. For a larger packet of food you may even be able to get a gold ring—from those murderous Ukrainian thugs in black uniforms, the ones who have already struck down so many good Poles.

The little bridge we are crossing is built over the Bug River, which bends around the small city of Malkinia. From here on, the road is paved. We pass two, three people. One in a conductor's uniform is leaning over the handlebars of his bicycle. Hey, look—there's a world out here, and people ride bicycles here in this world. We make a turn at the first building we approach and pass through the open gate.

We'll have to wait. Not all of our boards are ready yet. Schiffner, without his whip here, turns to the guards: "Okay, guards, listen, you stay here while we go away for a while, and this is no time for any of you to come up with any crazy ideas. You know what you'll get."

Both Schiffner and Bredow go into a two-story brick building on the other side of the street. It is just as isolated as the little sawmill on this side of the street. According to a small oval sign made of tin, the building houses a post office. "Where are those two going?"

The old fox from the Blue unit sticks his lower lip out: "Visiting the ladies—it's a post office, but the *Fräuleins* are not just there to sell stamps, and the supervisor's even got vodka and gourmet food."

We return, frozen stiff from the speedy drive back to the camp. I can't even eat, and right after roll call I lie down in my bunk. Catching cold. Karl's got the same thing. Not long and I'm burning up with fever. I wake up during the night shivering.

At morning roll call, rain beating down on our shorn heads, I lick my feverish lips and hear that today, Sunday, we will only work in the morning, and the afternoon will be free. It is the first time since Christmas that we have had at least a half day off . . .

As if an evil spirit had whispered in Miete's ear that we—Karl and I—are in awful shape, he comes and gets us to help out with the grading work at the sorting site. With an aloof, watery gaze, he waits until we join up, and then he turns away. So aloof on the outside, while waiting intently on the inside.

We drag ourselves back and forth with litters full of heavy wet sand. They are filled at the higher end of the site and dumped at the lower. Then we go back up again, and back down. The wind is driving the heavy, unending rain almost horizontally across the site and carrying with it fine sand that sticks to your drenched face. It invades your nose and mouth and eyes, works its way into the skin on your back, under the carrying straps, and hisses past your ears. A new round. I lean toward the man holding the litter, and as I shakily try to stand up with my load I can feel the rising fever hammering away inside my head. I paw the wet mushy sand and hardly notice the whiplash that drives me on. I lick my lips, and my mouth fills with sand. Sand, nothing but sand—this sand is probably from over there, fine, mixed with ashes.

How much longer—back and forth—really, how much longer? Even you are waiting, just waiting. You're dead anyway, but somehow you just can't die. Choronzycki, he was able to die honorably, and the man who stabbed Max Biala, the SS officer. What are you afraid of anyway? Of the moment when I am naked. There, you see, you've been here too long, you've been waiting too long, seen too much . . .

❖

The Key to the Munitions Depot

Finally, in the thoroughly warmed air of an advancing spring, the carousel in my head that was brought on by "Treblinka" has come to a stop. My ears are still ringing a little, but I no longer have to concentrate so much on keeping my balance. Most important of all, my thoughts are beginning to hold together again. Karl and I were struck by typhus at the very same time. Even in this respect we are twins. And now everyone's saying that we were bitten by one and the same louse. I don't know how long it has been since I survived my crisis in the sick bay—maybe three, maybe four weeks. Where my memory fails, others are filling me in.

That evening, when Robert examined us, I was still able to hear him saying: "Of course you'll stay on your feet as long as you can. But I'll check with Rybak to see when there might be a place for you."

During the first couple of days, we took our temperature—102, 104. On the third day, when the mercury crept up over 104 degrees, Karl hurled the thermometer at the wall of the barracks: "There now, at least we won't have to bother with that thing anymore." He had picked up the thermometer in Barracks B. It was thicker and more imposing than the one they had shoved under my arm at home whenever I had tonsillitis.

"You've got to, you've got to—just one more day . . ." David kicked me so that I stood up straight whenever a death's-head cap approached. And then he would pour tea down my throat again and make me gulp down pills. God knows where he ever came across these things in camp, and what he had to pay to get them.

On the eighth day of raging fever the struggle was over. There was no more swearing at me to hold on. That evening my tongue shot out of my open mouth, and I couldn't get it back in again.

Then the one thing I had to do was to get through evening roll call. At formation someone behind me held out his arm and the palm of his hand in such a way that I could lean back against him. From the front you couldn't tell what was happening.

"How many?" Rybak motioned to me in the sick bay. He sat there, knees spread, in a coat that used to be white. I answered with my fingers: eight days. "Well, tomorrow you're going to be having your first critical day. It's already started. I've got a bed opening up today, just under Karl. So I'll see you tomorrow morning—early."

I dragged myself back to my bunk in the barracks and thought to myself that I had too much stubble for one of Miete's super rounds in the sick bay. The rest of the men agreed, and we all set to work on my unshaven face. Hans held me, Robert soaped my face, Rudi shaved me, and I swore and called them sons of bitches.

In those days everything the organizing committee and the people around Galewski had devised was working. Now that Zelo was gone, our Rudi, who had risen to the rank of lieutenant during his military service, had begun to take part in the deliberations. Rudi Masarek didn't tell Karl and me a thing, because we were suffering from "Treblinka." He didn't say anything to the others either.

One day little Edek dashed by the door of the munitions depot and shoved a metal fragment into the lock. The munitions depot was directly accessible from the SS barracks. Actually, it was a concrete block to which wooden barracks were attached on both sides. SS living quarters, the weapons store, the dining hall, the kitchen— everything was under one roof. Only a very few of the Court Jews had access to this area: the singer, Salwe, little Edek, the younger cleaning boy, Heniek, approximately fifteen years old, the older cleaning boy, the nefarious Chaskel, and the man responsible for carrying out the garbage and taking care of the horses, wagons, and stalls.

When the SS found that they couldn't open the door, they called the locksmiths. The locksmiths tried the key, checked the lock, rattled the door, and finally explained that they would not be able to fix it on site and would have to take the door down and back to the workshop.

The whole thing was staged in much the same way as the escape of the two men who were smuggled out of Treblinka in the "reverse transport." When the locksmiths in the workshop again checked to see why the key would not fit into the lock, one of them hit it with his hand and screamed, the key fell from the workbench to the ground, one, two men bent over to get it, bumped into each other, felt for the key, and the others stood around and watched. Everyone was shouting and chattering away incomprehensibly in Yiddish, and by the time one of them stood up, key in hand, exclaiming *schojn*, "great," the imprint of the key had already been made *schon schojn* right under the watchful eyes of the SS.

About three days later, when I was lying on the lower bunk with my head directly up against the kitchen wall, one of the upper bunks opened up. Rybak had me moved up right next to Karl. My eyes opened from time to time, and I recognized Rybak's old smock. I didn't even feel the needle. I didn't once think it could've been the infirmary injection. Another time Cescha's round face, with little dimples in her cheeks, rose over the upper bunk, and her hands held a bowl out under my chin. "Rice soup—Bredow ordered it himself when he heard you two were sick—and here's a bottle of tea."

Slowly I began to come around. I managed to get a little soup down. It was different from the soup we got in our mess. It was a lot better. I suspected that Rybak was giving me part of the soup he always got from the Ukrainian mess.

From time to time, more in a dream state than in a state of consciousness, I was aware of Rudi straightening my bunk. Most of all I remember David's pale, bony face—the time he put two small shriveled apples into my hand, the way he kneeled on my bunk, leaned over me, kissed my forehead, and was gone. Two wrinkled old apples, so small that they could both fit into the palm of one hand, and a kiss on the forehead instead of a blow to the back of the neck. The kiss almost felt like a blow, being so rare, so remarkable. I couldn't have known then that this midday break was meant to be our last farewell. Everything had been set for that afternoon, and none of the men in the sick bay, nor any of the truly weak characters, nor the traitors, of course, were to know.

According to accounts given by the boys who worked in the SS barracks, there were two crates among the various small crates in the munitions depot that obviously contained hand grenades. After they had carried the two crates out, hidden under a heap of garbage, and brought them to the workshops in a wheelbarrow, the men with military experience determined that the hand grenades had no triggers. Either the triggers were being stored somewhere else in the munitions depot or they were being kept at an entirely different location. It was not possible for any of the older men, who knew about these things, to get into the SS barracks. At that time the organizing committee was being led by Kapo Kurland and a still weakened Galewski, while Rakowski, still functioning as camp elder, played a more or less passive role, moved more by the course of events than by his own will. It was decided that the hand grenades would be returned immediately and that the boys would be trained and the plans would be put off until they were again able to gather sufficient courage. They would wait for another Monday when there would be large amounts of garbage and debris to be cleared out of the barracks with wheelbarrows. The grenades were returned. Those of us lying in sick bay, Karl and I included, sensed nothing out of the ordinary when we heard the whistle for that evening's roll call.

On the sixth day my physical strength was beginning to return. Rybak helped me wash and shave. It was remarkable to see someone in Treblinka with such strong, clean hands. The next day, immediately after reveille, I fold my blankets, get dressed, and walk over to Rybak, who is sitting at his small desk facing the window with his back to the passageway between the bunks. He can see that I want to say something more than a simple farewell:

Doctor, I know that I shouldn't keep addressing you so formally, always using *Sie* and never *Du*, but that's the way it is when I'm talking to Galewski, Kurland, and you. I can't help it. In this camp, I say *Sie* to the three of you. I use *Sie* when I talk to Kapo Blue, but for an entirely different reason. I know that I shouldn't thank you, doctor. But please tell me why, when Bredow had Cescha bringing me things from the German mess, you kept giving me part of your Ukrainian soup too. And why do some of you not like me? Am I supposed to be something better? And others, the older ones especially, treat me as if—well, act as if I were their firstborn, the one who's supposed to have things better, or God knows what . . .

I don't get a single word of this out. But in exactly that same cadence, I pull on Rybak's soiled smock, somehow smiling, because Rybak is smiling a little too. After morning roll call I am confronted with my box in Barracks A.

The next day, as Karl left the sick bay, Kapo Rakowski was shot—the strongman Rakowski, for whom Lalka and a few of the others had a certain grudging respect. The Ukrainian guards had a kind of admiration for him because of his daring speculation, and we, in our never-ending game, had pinned many of our hopes on him.

On my own, I can recall the following scene rather clearly: Just as we were marching down to the mess for our midday break, Miete was leading Rakowski—who towered over him—past us and up to the "infirmary." This time he had a small escort of guards with him. Supposedly they had searched Rakowski's bedroll, and the other things in his bunk, and found large amounts of money and gold. But it looked as if they had just been waiting for the right moment. At a special roll call, the little barrel-shaped staff sergeant Stadie demonstrated what he could do when called upon to fill in for the vacationing Küttner and Franz. Full of rage, he snorted. His cheeks swelled, making his small eyes look all the more evil: "Anyone found with as little as a penny will be severely punished!"

"In spite of all that, he's just here as a substitute, and he's playing the meanest of games," Hans notes, giving the convalescent Karl a good kick in the rear to keep him standing up straight, so that he doesn't attract attention as they march off.

"Galewski and Kurland don't think they know anything specifically. It's just that they're getting suspicious, and they have to reassure themselves from time to time." Since Rudi has started taking part in committee meetings he often delivers himself of such intimations, casually, as if he had just let them slip out. He can't keep completely silent. For our part we know that we must not ask him too much.

"It's possible that the staff sergeant felt the need to take a preventive measure while Lalka and Kiewe, both pillars of Treblinka, are away."

"Or maybe the Little Barrel staff sergeant did it to show the Doll Franz how diligent he is. While he's on vacation his favorite gets done away with."

"Moniek, one of the Court Jews, thinks there must be something to this. He's the one who's most afraid of the three stool pigeons here."

"And what about the guards who disappeared from camp right after Rakowski and have since been replaced?"

In this phase of indecision and misgiving, a few large transports arrive. They are the most miserable of all the transports that have ever arrived in Treblinka. No baggage whatsoever. Tatters and rags instead of clothing. More dead and half dead in the cattle cars than ever before. Only a few who stir at all. Nonetheless, the SS select a few of them to replenish the decimated ranks of the work crews—so that they'll have more slaves for the extensive rebuilding and expansion of Treblinka, so that the SS Treblinka Special Commando will have proof of its vast accomplishments, so that for the next transports the path from the train station will lead past beds of flowers through a parklike setting to the "bath."

But the overlords and the master executioners don't realize what legacy these transports full of survivors of the Warsaw Ghetto Uprising bring with them, and how the chosen ones pass it on to the gravediggers in Treblinka.

As David Brat listens to the newcomers, the blue of his eyes grows brighter than the blue of a late summer sky. The Warsaw Ghetto no longer exists. In its place only rubble and ruins remain. The underground smuggled weapons into the ghetto. The Jews rose up. They all knew they had nothing but Treblinka before them. So the few who had escaped from Treblinka had succeeded, at least there, in letting the world know. In the end the Germans had been forced to bring in tanks and heavy guns in order to put down the uprising, which included women, the elderly, and children.

The dead and the dying wounded were thrown into cattle cars. Then the Germans crammed in as many more as they could still capture. And this is how these people were brought to us in Treblinka—in stifling heat, shot, bayoneted, suffocated, bloated, decaying. The incineration pits at the "infirmary" were overflowing with distended corpses, and everything in this inferno melted into an immense glutinous mass.

The transports brought nothing for speculation from the ruined Warsaw Ghetto. Nothing moved from hand to hand, not one slice of bread, not one pair of pants, not one chunk of soap. But from mouth to mouth, from one mind to another, the legacy was passed on: You who are faithful out of conviction as well as practice, Talmudists as well as nonbelievers, businessmen as well as tradesmen, craftsmen as well as shopkeepers, brokers, hustlers, crooks, and thieves

—each of you, cast off the last remains of this life, give up hoping that you will be the last to escape this naked death. Show the world and yourselves . . .

After a few days there are no longer any signs of the Warsaw Ghetto in Treblinka. But it is clear that extensive construction and repair are under way inside the camp and out. Barracks are being fixed up, roads resurfaced, grounds leveled and finished with gravel, smaller areas and embankments sodded. The cultivated field outside the fence has been enlarged. "Spanish Riders"—iron tank traps— have been set up at the edge of the field, between the watchtowers, with an expanse of barbed wire on both sides.

To clear the woods around the perimeter of the camp—that's our main task now. Felled trees are hauled into camp and chopped into firewood. As spring becomes summer without transports, the greatest concentration of activity in the first camp moves down to the grounds behind the Ukrainian barracks, to the lumberyard. Those of us from Barracks A work there, along with other commando units who had previously worked at the sorting site. Idyllic mounds of freshly sawn and split firewood grow up and shine out from among the towering pines that have not been felled. A path runs along one side of the lumberyard and leads up to the main gate of the second camp. Though it is some seventy meters away, the gate is clearly visible from our work site. Here we deliver what wood is needed in that part of the camp. No one from over there is allowed out to work by the SS. The main work in the second camp still consists of digging up and incinerating the bodies from old transports.

Masquerade

While I was sick with typhus, Lalka had two foxes, a few squirrels and pigeons, and a variety of other small animals delivered to Treblinka. The carpenters and cabinetmakers were ordered to build a camp zoo beyond the fence in the vicinity of our kitchen, at the point where a path leads off to the Ukrainian barracks. Pigeon lofts were built on the roofs of both the SS barracks and the headquarters building. Lalka assigned our Rudi the task of overseeing all of Treblinka's animal population. In this capacity Rudi suggested that some of the feed—pigeon seed and the like—be stored in the small dry cellar abutting the munitions depot. This habitat, also known as Zoo Corner, is not the only innovation at Treblinka: a stable, a pig sty, and a small chicken yard have also been added.

Perhaps bored because of a lack of real work in Treblinka, perhaps distressed at the inauspicious news from the outside, the SS are looking for diversion, and Lalka, of course, is the most inventive of them all. We all knew that he was interested in music, and someone alerted him to the fact that Arthur Gold, a famous Warsaw musician, had arrived on one of the last transports. Lalka, "the Doll," had Gold brought out and gave him the assignment of forming a small orchestra in Treblinka. There are certainly enough musicians here: both of the red-haired Schermanns, the only siblings here, Salwe, the tenor, little Edek with his accordion, and many others.

When our gentlemen and masters returned from vacation, they brought various musical instruments with them, including trumpets and clarinets. We had already taken enough violins off the transports. Küttner brought sheet music with German songs and marches. Still Franz outdid him: he had somehow found a drum. But that wasn't all. Franz had left on vacation a master sergeant and returned

a second lieutenant. Küttner-Kiewe is still first sergeant. He express-
es his rage accordingly.

At the earliest opportunity, Second Lieutenant Kurt Hubert
Franz introduces himself, in particular to Sergeant Küttner, and to
us as well, as the deputy camp commandant: "I want to hear voices
singing, a robust choir of all you shorn heads. Gold, these carpenters here will build you a small podium, and you and your musicians will play as we form up and when we file off, and there will be
an additional musical offering in the evening after roll call. Who of
you has had any experience writing rhymes and text?" There will be
someone—you can find anything you're looking for in Treblinka . . .
"Right. You will write the lyrics to the melody that Gold is going to
compose, and this song will describe life and work in Treblinka. It
will be your hymn, you monkeys, you dreamers. It will be Treblinka's hymn. You've got two days, and if you don't finish it by then,
we won't waste any more room and board on you. And to provide
the finishing touch, tailors will sew special uniforms for the musicians."

Now as they march out of the camp, their shovels slung over their
shoulders, it would be difficult to recognize the elegant gentlemen
who were formerly employed in the "department store." Their worn
boots are a dusty gray, shirts hang loosely over their pants like underwear, their faces are sunburned and sweaty, their hands completely
callused. SS men and guards are walking along the top of the embankment. Here below, the work crew on the tracks is stumbling out
through the gate. "Treblinka!" comes a shout from the embankment.
"Hey, let's hear it, Treblinka! *Dawaj, Treblinka!*" the Ukrainians are
screaming, and once more the herd down below with its shovels raises its voice in song, the song of Treblinka. They sang it at morning
roll call, and after roll call while marching off to work; and on their
way back they will sing it two or three more times, and then again at
evening roll call:

> Ever onward, firm in step and gait,
> hearts full and brave,
> they march
> to work that will not wait.

Today we are Treblinka,
whatever is our fate.
Today we are Treblinka,
to work that will not wait.

When we hear our honored master's call
our ranks we swiftly fill,
to work and to obey
our solemn duty one and all.

Our work, our lives are one,
to Treblinka we are bound,
we shall strive and strive still more
to work and to obey until the task is done.

One hot, sunny day follows another, tar drips from barrack rooftops, and grains of sand blow in from over there, from the death camp. A suffocating heat has settled in over Treblinka. The smallest wound, every little scratch, festers immediately because death has already permeated everything you touch. Your legs swell with water, and you have Treblinka in your blood. Do you know how you can tell? Somewhere on your body, usually on your legs, you will find a small white blister with a black spot in the middle. In a few days this will become an oozing abscess; a second one, a third, and a fourth will follow. If you press a finger into your leg the indentation will stay behind as if it had been made in mud.

A summer without transports inspires new ideas in Lalka. Evening roll call is over, the sun is setting and Lalka, his head lowered in a casually imperious stance, listens as the sorrowful Polish song "Gorlau" rises from five hundred throats. "You monkeys, every time you take a shit in those two latrines, you're in there so long you might as well be holding some kind of conference." Lalka looks around for Tölpel, a little fellow whose bald head may no longer be quite in order. As he's standing there cringing at attention, his pants hanging rumpled over his crooked legs, Lalka takes his measure. "Yes, you're the one."

A Ukrainian guard manages to dig up an old robe from one of the transports. The SS men, one after the other, add to the costume.

Topping off the black robe, which reaches all the way down to his ankles, is a tall rabbi's hat. The hat is decorated with a shiny half moon, and the small hand, which has probably never been made into a fist, is now wielding a heavy whip. "A sign will be put on each of the latrines: Two minutes the limit for shitting here. Take any longer, and you're out on your ear!"

Lalka is hardly finished with his rhyme before Bredow hangs a large kitchen clock around the neck of the "Shit-Kapo." His mouth hanging half open, the little man in the long black robe listens respectfully as he is given his instructions: "So as soon as someone goes into the latrine, you check your clock, and he's got to be finished in two minutes. You are now the grand sovereign over everyone and their shit.

"Now we've taken care of the upper camp. We'll need one more for the lower latrine." The SS men go through the ranks and pick out a big, clumsy fellow. Any moment now the head, with its bumpy face, may simply roll off his shoulders, while his arms and legs dangle around aimlessly, looking as if they don't belong to the rest of his body. After this Shit-Kapo is suited up in similar fashion, they fasten a wide leather belt like a corset around the midsection of his body so that he won't somehow break in two under his robe.

Ever since this day, you hear the most unusual screams coming from the latrine located next to the green fence around the "infirmary" in the upper camp: "*No jazda, wychodzic*—all right, outta there! *Panie, pan juz tu siedzi wiecej jak dve minuty*—sir, your two minutes are up—Mosche, if Lalka shows up . . ." The little caftan man, ornamented with his half moon, takes his work seriously. His brain is capable of nothing more. But who the hell knows—there may be something more than any of us had expected.

How are things in the lower camp latrine, thatched in straw like some idyllic hut? A hoarse monotone rules here: "All right, shit, shit *Chaverim*—my friends, but there are too many of you here. Kuba, *gaj rojs*—get out, or let's roll a cigarette! No tobacco? Then get out. Make room, there's a better guest," he greets Willy as he approaches, one of the Gold Jews.

Eight, ten naked bottoms are hanging over the long smelly pit in the half-dark shed. The hum of the flies only accentuates the sultry stillness. "Mietek bought a pack from Saschka early this morning. He'll give you something to smoke."

"*Na prawde*—really, Mietek? *No nech mie krew zaleje*—may blood flow over me, and I let him sit there without paying up."

Another voice chimes in: "They've got some kind of guns and ammunition in the little bunker next to the administration building, the same place they've got their booze."

"How the hell did you get in there? They keep a close eye on that place."

"Just take it easy, gentlemen. Everything will work out. Personally, I'm not in such a big hurry. If they promise they won't do anything worse than this to me, I'll be their crap sweeper until the end of the war, until they've shit out everything they've got. Shit-Kapo, that'll be a real career. Kapo for crap, it is now and will always be a job. My daddy and my mama—may the sand of Treblinka rest lightly over them—they knew what they were doing when they gave me this kisser and this body. The Almighty told them that there'd be some very hard times coming, and that they shouldn't make me handsome and able, then I wouldn't get married and cry over my wife and children at Treblinka."

Someone spits on the hard dirt floor. "The telephone checks are a bigger problem. Supposedly the telephone rings every hour, and they have to answer. Simcha was in the administration building delivering chairs and he heard something like that."

"Why are we making it so complicated for ourselves? Within ten minutes everything's got to be burning, and then who gives a shit what happens after that."

"Grischka, the little guard, is supposed to have found a pistol somewhere. Moniek was talking to him."

"How much is he asking?"

"Well, probably about a thousand soft ones . . ."

"He'll want hard ones—eyes."

"Two hundred fifty dollars in gold coins, and that's a lot even for Treblinka . . ."

"Don't worry about it."

With both hands the gloomy shit-master grabs onto the wide belt he was given by the SS at his inauguration. It is now being filled with gold dollars, rubles, and louis d'or, one coin after the other. The pendulous head looks out of the latrine entrance and across the hot black cinder surface of the assembly site: "Okay, okay, you sons of bitches, outta there. Your time's up—outta there!" We hear loud shouts and the crack of a whip. Just to be safe, the sovereign of the lower latrine bellows again but gradually stops banging his whip against the shed. He straightens his robe, pushes his tall rabbi's hat back, and carefully surveys the assembly site again: "You can stay where you are. He's already gone, turned off toward the upper camp."

At evening roll call Lalka announces a new plan for our entertainment: "Now that we're not working on Sunday afternoons, we'll have a little amusement, maybe a little cabaret—with music, singing, skits, boxing. The people down in the workshops are putting together a real boxing ring. It must be finished in two days. Dismissed!"

On a lovely Sunday afternoon we are all herded onto the assembly site in front of the boxing ring. The greenish black gentlemen sit down on chairs that have been set up in a half circle. The shorn heads, the bearers and loaders, tailors and shoemakers, carpenters and cabinetmakers, cooks and laundry maids, clerks and accountants, supervisors, medics, gravediggers—we all crowd in behind these gentlemen, surrounded by black mercenaries and riflemen. Treblinka is a world unto itself, isolated from the other world.

Arthur Gold and his boys, all in white jackets with large blue lapels, open the festivities with a march. Captain Stangl is sitting in an easy chair in the middle of his men, tapping his foot and keeping time, gently beating the top of his boot with his riding whip. A flourish: First Salwe the singer steps up and presents an Italian tarantella. He is followed by Treblinka's newest acquisition, a cantor, supposedly the best in Warsaw, who was taken off one of the last transports. He was trained in religious song but is also familiar with secular music. A tenor voice sends an aria from Verdi's *Tosca* rising high over the barracks, the green fence, and the twisted pines. But this voice cannot be compared with Salwe's full worldly tones. This voice comes from the temple and rises to dizzying heights with such ease because there is a bond between it and the Lord. We recognize his next song, an aria from Halevy's *Jewess*, and exchange knowing looks among ourselves: "Recha, I consecrate you in death . . ." After the song is over Stangl looks around. He is probably the only one of them who heard anything more in this song than the melody.

There is no applause, and Lalka interrupts the short pause: "Now let's have something lighter, something amusing—Willy, hey Willy!"

An articulated thought becomes the command that brings Lalka's favorite and inspired comic to the podium. He requests a newspaper from his audience and sits down on a chair, making himself comfortable, as if he had just eaten his midday meal. Then he spreads out the newspaper and begins to read out loud to himself: "Mama, coffee!" he yells, looking out over the top of his borrowed glasses in the direction of the kitchen. Willy keeps reading through to the last page, to the announcements about who's getting married and who's getting divorced. He recalls that he knew them when they were still single. Suddenly, with heightened concentration, he moves a little forward on his chair: "Treblinka Spa. Visit the new health resort Treblinka—located in lovely surroundings, deep forests, fresh air, wholesome climate, special medical care, diet, modern medical facilities for more serious illnesses, zoo, chapel, concerts, traditional races, and other athletic activities, direct railway connections, comfortable accommodations at reasonable prices—and all this with absolutely no spa tax."

I am standing at one end of the half circle, and I can see the faces of the SS. Laughter has come over many of their faces, even Franz's, but still it all looks forced. Küttner slides around uneasily on his chair; Stangl raises his eyebrows, and his mouth forms an indecipherable smile. David's words, whispered into my ear, sound almost like an incantation: "Even more shame and humiliation, until finally no one here can take it anymore."

"Shit-Kapos into the ring!" Sepp Hirtreiter leaps up from his chair.

Franz turns around in surprise. It looks as if he's unhappy that he didn't come up with the idea first. But this expression quickly fades: "Y-e-e-s, the Shit-Kapos!"

The caftans are removed. The big one doesn't have any underpants, so they roll up his pants legs around his knees. The little one is wearing two pairs of underpants, one over the other, and as they raise his arm in the familiar athletic salute, he arches his frail body, covered as it is with insect bites. Meanwhile Sepp has gotten two bottles of soda water from the SS barracks. "The lower latrine is overweight!"

"Each round will last for two shit-minutes!"

Gong! The first round. The big guy drags himself to the middle of the ring on his two tree trunks, and the hands inside the boxing gloves make a challenging motion: Okay boy, let's go. The little one gathers himself and raises his hands too: You, if you lay a hand on me, I'll . . . ! And the big guy responds again with his arms and his giant gloves: And why should I hit you? The SS get up from their chairs and shout: "Let's go, go!"

The fighter from the lower latrine opens his mouth, his ears sticking out even more than usual, and leans over: "All right, hit me." The fighter from the upper latrine jumps up as high as he can, but he still can't reach his opponent. With both little hands he boxes the big man in the stomach. The big man shoves his glove into the face of the little one and pushes him away into the ropes. Gong!

When they give the little one something to drink, the soda water comes foaming out of his nose. The band plays a flourish, and Treblinka cheers.

Lalka's next idea eclipses everything that he has done up until now. "You're a bunch of real men, aren't you? And we've got some women here too. We're going to have a wedding, a genuine wedding. All right, two of you step forward, or I'll do the choosing myself. Then we'll arrange for you to be alone. In the back of the barracks, next to the plumber's shop and the forge, we'll have a special room for all newlyweds at Treblinka. And what will we call it? Of course— the Wedding Barracks!"

That very next Sunday a small wedding procession walks from the living quarters to the assembly site. Of course, it is Chaskel, cleaning boy and informer, and little Perele, who is not exactly ugly but certainly plain. They have never had to touch a corpse. Both of them have enough to eat, and Chaskel even has enough to drink. Maybe that's his reward for doing a good job. In return for his good work he gets their dregs. But there is no pomp, no religious ceremony, no band, no attendance requirement for the entire camp. Since Franz's promotion—which also means that he has become the deputy camp commandant, Stangl's deputy, that is—Stangl apparently believes that Franz's ideas have become a little too inspired. Of course he will allow Franz to follow through with his plan, but without the fanfare and pageantry, and without the other SS.

On hot evenings, when no one can stand to stay inside, before twilight and before the signal is given for lights out, a kind of promenade takes place on the assembly site behind the barbed wire. The women come. Some just stand around, others parade arm in arm with their men around the assembly site, and some sit down along the back wall of the barracks. Near the latrine, under the enormous beech tree that had continued to grow in Treblinka and was providing comfort on this hot summer evening, a small group gathers and talks. Maybe someone is asking if anyone has served in the military and is familiar with hand grenades. They—should the Germans win the war—will make a museum out of Treblinka, and organize excursions. Lalka is supposed to have come up with this idea just recently. And then they'll really take good care of us. Actually we, the ones they've selected, already have the worst behind us. So we'll survive, survive until the end. They'll leave us our lives—this life.

✿

Camouflage

Half of the camp is dragging around with infections, getting weaker and weaker. Robert is on the bunk next to mine and so infirm that he can hardly sit up anymore. Rudi's fever will not go away. Only Karl and I are so brown from the wind and the sun that we are ashamed to have the others see us here on these bunks. We have just managed to come up with some summer clothing. A light jacket over linen slacks, complete with shiny spots from ham, vodka, resin, and fresh pine needles—around the pockets, on the backside, on the lower arms and the knees. And now, in the camouflage commando, this is what has become of the two fine and dandy swells from Haberdashery Type I.

Everything, all of the changes in assignment and work units, seemed to take place so naturally and without design. We tell the men we don't trust that we've taken on this heavy work so that we won't have to look death in the face, take it up in our hands, always inhaling its stench. For the ones we do trust, it's enough to indicate that Kleinmann, the foreman of the camouflage commando, wants us there, as do many of the others. After we had been working with the camouflage unit inside the camp at the lumberyard for a few days, Kleinmann unobtrusively introduced us to his boss. He had waited for the appropriate moment, when Sergeant Sydow—a short little guy but very tough, with an unbelievable appetite for alcohol, a dockworker from Hamburg—had drunk so much that he felt himself three times as grand when he was able to nod in assent.

The camouflage unit is the only one of the old work squads that still has enough real work to do. There is so much exterior and interior fencing that there are always repairs to be made. And if there are no repairs, then the camouflage unit is well suited for the forestry work in the vicinity of the camp—for clearing and cutting. Several times a day, under the supervision of the guards and little Sydow, some part of the twenty-five man unit has to go out into the forest, climb into the trees, harvest large branches, and carry them back into the camp, where they will be used for repairs. The other part of the unit straightens and firms up the posts, tightens the barbed wire, and weaves the new pine boughs into the fence until there are no longer any gaps in the dense green wall. We know how to carry our two or three straps in such a way that everyone immediately understands: We are the camouflage unit. In the forest we bundle the pine boughs we have harvested and then strap them to our backs.

The contact with nature outside the camp, as well as the work on the fencing, really has made something special of us. When we return to the camp we smell like the forest, we have fresh green on our sweaty clothing, and in the evening we dump pine needles out of our shoes and onto our bunks.

From climbing into the trees and breaking off branches, Karl and I have scratches on our hands and faces. Building on our experience inside the camp, we now begin training for advanced speculation and smuggling. We learn to hide money all over our bodies—taped in armpits, tucked in the heels of our shoes, sewn into belts. And luck has been with us: Yesterday we took a chance and simply stuffed the money into our pockets. But today, with each of us carrying a ten-ruble gold piece in his mouth, is the very day when they decide to make a spot check of the camouflage unit as it passes out through the front gate. Well, Küttner-Kiewe will have to drill our stomachs open if he wants to get anything out of me and Karl.

The gate opens, and the work crew, straps slung over their shoulders, march out of the camp. And now everything depends on whether or not our boss suffers a bout of sobriety. We all know that if that were to happen we would be picking up nothing but pine branches, and there wouldn't be the slightest thought of speculation. But Sydow seems to be having one of his really good days today. He is herding us through the forest, parallel with the Białystok road, which can be seen through the trees. "Si-i-inng Treblinka!"

What, Shorty wants us to sing? That way the speculators will find us. Despite strict prohibition and bitter experience, flat-footed Adrian exchanges a few words with a ragged speculator who has just put in an appearance nearby. The guards notice this violation and beat

Adrian until there would be nothing left to shovel up if this were any other man. But this is Adrian, also known as Dr. Adrian, and it is impossible to imagine this unit of camouflage cons without him. Yesterday afternoon he got twenty-five lashes across his backside from Shorty, and a few across the face with the handle of the whip.

But Adrian just took the beating in stride and went on to speculate a packet of food from a guard in the woods. At the same time he was grandly conning everyone who dealt with him. For their part, the objects of his con jobs responded with a lash of the whip. But it is unlikely that their blows pained Adrian as much as their losses did them. Immune to the lashes, which he attracts like a magnet, he wades through the sand on feet almost as broad as flippers. For some strange reason the whip seems to have no effect on him. Not a drop of blood is drawn. I only once saw him spit out a tooth.

Little Adrian, with his rather large turned-up nose, doesn't look particularly rugged, but his body seems to be made only of sinew and calluses. And it must be those calluses that are protecting his very broad rear end. With an agility that is surprising for a man of his stature, he scrambles to the top of a tree and is finished breaking off branches before any of the rest of us. And then, whenever the opportunity presents itself, he's down on the ground stealing branches from the men who are still up in the tree. And this is so bad? Oy, Karol, Richard, where I come from it was bad to make off with the last tiny onion and a chunk of dry bread, but to get your branches swiped right out from under your nose! Adrian, doctor of speculation sciences, plods back to camp with his bundle on his back and cogitates. This evening in the barracks, for the piece of white bread, sausage, and bacon, for the small bottle of vodka he has under his shirt, or in his pants leg, he can expect no more than thirty soft ones—dollar bills. That's because the road crew commando was also out today picking up fieldstone. They were being supervised by our gentle Seidel and a relatively good group of guards, so they will certainly have brought back something to sell.

If he were to divide the whole thing into four portions, combining a smaller one with the bottle of vodka, then he could get ten soft ones for each portion. He could very likely get ten hard ones for the forty soft ones. The ten hard ones are actually one ten-dollar gold piece, also known as a small eye, which itself is one-half of a large

eye, the twenty-dollar gold coin that is the most valuable currency
on the Treblinka market. Or for ten soft ones he might get five little
pigs, a five, as the five-ruble gold piece is known.

No, Adrian decides otherwise. He does divide his take into four
small portions, where the sausage is no longer than the length of a
finger, but he will only sell two portions this evening, one for ten
soft ones and the other for five thousand Polish zloty, so he'll have
something to work with the next time he speculates with the guards.
Five thousand zloty do make a sizable bulge under your shirt, and it's
dangerous to be carrying around so much, but the guards sometimes
need zloty for direct purchases. They don't spend their dollars; they
hoard them. And from time to time the guards have been more
interested in zloty than dollars, and then—oy, oy, oy—did the zloty
ever rise against the dollar, over the period of a half day, from noon
until evening! Adrian won't sell the other two portions today.
Instead, he will hide them in his bunk until tomorrow. Maybe camouflage won't go out tomorrow, or maybe the Little Boss will have
his quarterly fit of sobriety and it won't be possible to speculate at
all. Then prices in the barracks will climb; they will climb in the
interval between evening roll call and lights out. The best deals are
made just before lights out. And what if Adrian ends up in the
"infirmary" tomorrow or suffers some other, similar end? Well, those
are simply the risks an entrepreneur has got to accept.

"Oy, oy, oy, Madagaskar . . ." In a spare, hoarse voice, Adrian
starts in on a sorrowful melody. There is a bitter smile on his face, a
grimace that is as much a part of Yiddish as masks are of the theater.
Instead of Erez, the Promised Land, they promised us a large, distant
island. There, instead of the flames of pogroms, we will find nothing
but the glow of the sun. They would take us to that island, and we
would be allowed to live and build our homes there . . .

Nothing works out, neither the journey to Madagascar nor Adrian's deals. During the night someone steals his wares. Adrian curses
the entire breathing population of Treblinka and suspects old
Jitzrock, the man who sleeps next to him and also works in the camouflage unit. Neither Adrian nor old Jitzrock, his face as red and raw
as a piece of uncooked meat, really believes that in the next few days
the camouflage commando will be subjected to the kind of strict
regime that's being rumored.

But they couldn't have been more wrong. Camouflage is divided into four groups, each with six members. Each group chooses a foreman. As soon as the commando unit is outside the camp, the foreman collects approximately the same amount of currency from each of his members. The four foremen then give their money to the tall and lanky Kuba, the only one who is authorized to deal with the guards, paying out money and receiving goods. There is no one better suited to this task than Kuba, who, with his refined, rather aloof voice, his reddish face and blond eyebrows, has perfected his act and is always able to achieve just the right tone of voice. As soon as he accepts the surreptitious delivery of goods, his job is done, and the foremen reappear on the scene. The others have continued to work, providing cover for the deal makers. First they set aside a portion for Kleinmann, their supervisor. Everything else is divided into four equal portions. Then each foreman returns to his group and just as covertly divides the quarter into six equal parts.

In the first few days of this iron regime, the camouflage commando finds itself in a terrible state. The guards lash out in a rage because suddenly it is impossible to overcharge for their wares. The tall and lanky Kuba, with his soft, fragile voice, is offering them ten dollars, and that's all anyone has. Adrian and old Jitzrock are getting double their share of blows, from the guards with their rifles, whips, and pieces of wood, and from workmates with their straps.

Over the next few days, in an attempt to starve out the camouflage unit, the guards stand around in the woods stuffing themselves full of bacon, ham, and sausage. There are two or three more hungry days. Then finally, as soon as we are outside the camp gate, the fat, always sweaty guard asks, as if nothing had transpired: "Okay, who's got the cash?"

Then Adrian answers, as if he were swearing a solemn oath in front of himself: "Well, who else, *panie*—sir, but big Kuba? He's always the one. Kuba does the deals . . ."

And who is this supervisor Kleinmann? Here is just one more example of the ambiguity that flourishes in Treblinka. To supervise vicious, hardened gangsters, smugglers who smuggle for good as well as for evil, they chose a man who had heretofore never let a single mean word pass his lips. His whip gets caught between his legs and trips him up, and he switches it into his other hand, embarrassed. In school he was a good, well-behaved pupil who always got good grades without being considered too studious or too groveling. In his private life he was probably a competent, responsible bureaucrat and the father of a good bourgeois family. He had been living with his wife and child somewhere in eastern Germany when, even before the war, the Nazis deported him as a Jew of Polish decent. Here in Treblinka the SS show him a certain grudging respect; the Malochers and Schlaumeiers of the camouflage commando ask his advice and always make sure he receives his portion of their wares. His authority is based on the naturally polite manner in which he mediates among members of the camouflage commando, and between the unit and our SS thug. And this little tough has his own reasons for being pleased with the likable gentleman with the round face and round eyeglasses.

Of late our little boss sometimes misses morning roll call. It seems that his alcoholic excesses have often continued late into the night. And while the camouflage commando stands at attention waiting for its little boss, Küttner, pencil and journal in hand, inspects the units as they march off to their assigned duties and yawningly notes: "Sergeant Sydow absent again . . ."

Apparently the SS is at a loss. Sydow knows too much about their dirty business. Maybe they are waiting for Sydow to do himself in, or hoping that the next time he goes on vacation they'll be able to decommission him the way they have decommissioned others.

Küttner sends the camouflage unit, without its boss, to do make-work on the inside fencing along the embankment near the tracks across from the arrival ramp. We are to check for loose barbed wire and gaps in the pine boughs. After about an hour we see Sydow approaching us, accompanied by Boelitz. "You swine, my dear, sweet camouflage . . ." It is obvious that our little boss is in the throes of a powerful hangover. He is arrogant and reckless. He falls off the ramp onto the tracks but gets up immediately. This seems almost a matter of course. He can't fall over, since he's so small and bottom heavy, like one of those little dolls that always rights itself.

Boelitz jumps down after him, and he tells Boelitz that he doesn't need him anymore and he should go to hell. And he doesn't need any first sergeant anyway, or any other kind of caretaker running after him either. Then, to prove his point, he pulls Boelitz up in an affable display of muscle. Standing not much taller than his superior's waistline, he picks the officer up by the belt with one hand and deliberately sets him back down again.

When he notices our group up on the embankment, he begins to spew forth: "You dogs, you gang of swindlers, you haven't done a damn thing, and it's already . . ." He takes out his pocket watch and gapes at it for a while . . . "Heinriich, come down here," he yells to Kleinmann. "Closer, that's right, like that . . ." Some time passes. Shorty stands frozen in place, his head resting on Kleinmann's chest. Standing on the embankment above, the guards laugh and scream, trying to determine how soundly he's sleeping.

At the far end of the square in front of the train station, Kiewe's high cap shoots by. Kleinmann notes this movement immediately. "Sergeant, sir, sir." Kleinmann takes one step back. Sydow stumbles forward but still doesn't fall.

"Heinriich, you woke me up for him? Karl, Richard! Come here—you're two fine boys—tell me, who's responsible for this war?" Without waiting for an answer, he goes on: "Well, I'll tell you. It's not you. It's those English Jews, and we're gonna get 'em all here. Right. They're coming to Treblinka." He turns his back to us and spreads his arms: "Everything will be ready—this is going to be a real train station—there'll be signs—there'll be a big clock up on top of the barracks—the Blue commando will get railway uniforms—your Kapo'll have a red supervisor's cap. And you dogs, let's get to work!" He bellows but then immediately reverts to a more comradely tone. "Heinriich, we only work for a half day today. It's Sunday, and we only work until half past eleven—but we work like the devil! Adrian, get those saws hot, hot, hot—and at half past eleven, out—then we'll all sit down together and sing, we'll sing pious songs."

A few days ago, little by little, in small groups, they delivered about three thousand people. Maybe they were closing down or reducing the size of one of the smaller penal camps. Maybe the infantry was making a sweep of the surrounding woods and shipping off everyone they caught to Treblinka, to be burned. Wasted figures in prisoner's jackets, reckless speculators, and finally, in the last of the cars, gypsies. The flames of the "infirmary" fires were being fanned again, and we could tell by the rags that were being thrown in to fuel the inferno that these people had come from many different backgrounds and many different countries. Might this perhaps be an indication of a new phase in Treblinka's historical function? Hasn't everything been organized and prepared for new deliveries? What if they should actually win the war, or what if it simply never ends? Will Treblinka function as a crematorium for whatever refuse might exist on the fringes of civilization? But why are they wandering around so apathetically, and muttering to themselves "Everything shit, shit, shit"?

In just a few more days we will do what the world is waiting for us to do. Through the darkness in our barracks I can see David's bright blue eyes and the arthritic fingers on his raised hands. As I return to my bunk I can hear him whispering: "There's a piece of sausage, two rolls, and a bottle of vodka—they want ten soft ones. Mosche, come on, fifty-fifty, but hurry up or it'll be gone."

Rudi Masarek is holding court over at my bunk: "There are seven hundred of us in all. Two hundred over there, and here, in the first camp, about five hundred. And do you know how many of the five hundred have been in the military and know how to use a weapon? According to our count, it's somewhat more than forty men."

"Did you say there were two small cases of hand grenades, about six rifles, and a pistol for Kurland? That's not even going to last for five minutes."

"Wait, wait." Standa Lichtblau, who's stopped off at our bunk, interrupts Hans. "What about the gasoline, an entire tankful, and the pump? A rag soaked in gasoline and set on fire, a few leaky gas cans, and in this weather that should be enough for half of Treblinka. It's too bad that I won't see it burn. It's about fifty meters from the garage to the pump. My dear boss has told me that the pump's mine. Okay, I'll take the pump. That'll be my solo appearance—as one huge, flaming torch, in memory of my wife and daughter . . ." Standa chops each of his words, one after the other, like everyone else from Moravian Ostrów. His big strong teeth show as he speaks. But you can't tell whether he's smiling or trying to hold something back.

These days the commando unit responsible for the upkeep of the entire camp, and especially for the appearance of all of the newly built facilities, is by chance working very close to the ramparts again. *"Na, na—wszystko tu sprzatac—*let's get that cleaned up, you sons of

bitches—be ready—*przyjaciele, Chaverim,* friends—next Monday—
get over here with your rakes—get moving, at four o'clock in the
afternoon—over there, level it off with those rakes—signaled by
hand grenades—*predzej,* get moving with that litter—set everything
on fire . . ." The foreman of the maintenance commando is shouting
in Yiddish and Polish. If we can hear them yelling across the ramparts from Camp 2, "C'mon, pick up those bones," then they must
be able to hear us too. Finally the response comes from over there:
"Got it!"

Carrying bundles on our backs, camouflage commando returns
to the camp. As we approach, the resinous fragrance of the pine needles is suppressed by the stifling air of the camp. As the work crew is
hiking down the side road toward the tracks, we hear voices yelling,
and shots ring out. In the sand by the road we get rid of the goods
we've been carrying. And by the time we reach the gate to Camp 2
everything has quieted down again. Along the way we find out what
happened. They executed the entire woodcutter commando for
speculating with the Ukrainians. Did Küttner just find out the
Ukrainians aren't carrying water around in their canteens, or did he
smell the meat?

The gate to Camp 2 is opened halfway. The SS order us to bring
our bundles in. I cross the boundary into the horrifying factory of
death. Even if they decide to keep me here now, I will only stay until
the day after tomorrow. A group of people appear, and I recognize
Zelo among them. The fires have turned his complexion brown; he's
gaunt but still dignified. Everyone here is dressed in rags. Zelo smiles
at me in silence. Behind him there is a brick building with a steep
roof. This must be the entrance to the gas chambers. So the Pipeline
doesn't lead directly into the entrance after all. It stops just short of
it. Behind the building, and off to the side, I believe I can see steel
rails. Is that the incineration grate? The path leading up to the
entrance is on a slight incline. The sandy surface is firmly packed.
There are trees on both sides, forming a kind of boulevard. There are
blocks of green grass everywhere, beds of bright-colored stone, sandy
pathways, ashen gray and yellow. Then another familiar face appears:
Adasch, the former foreman of Barracks A, yells something to Zelo
and a few of the others, in Yiddish, so that we all understand: "What
are you waiting for? Everything's finished, isn't it?"

2 August 1943

On Sunday afternoon, our time off, we carry our blankets out onto the assembly site to air them in the sun. This is the first time we've done this. One of us started, and before long the entire square was covered with blankets. "What do you think, shall we air out our blankets?"

"Man, are you crazy? For the last night? Here, lie down and take a rest."

"No, after tomorrow we'll have plenty of time for lying around and resting."

"What we really should do is make an accounting. Just how many people have been murdered here?"

"Well, let's see, by the time we arrived, they had already done away with two, maybe three hundred thousand people. In the first few months everything was in high gear: on one day they killed ten thousand, the next five thousand, and then fifteen thousand."

"And for how long were they operating at capacity?"

"We got here on October 10. And the stream of transports didn't let up until the second half of December. Then in January, the lice-infested trains from Grodno and Białystok—and in March, the splendid Balkans. Then the transports after the Warsaw Uprising, and finally, the remains from whatever other camps there were, mostly crooks and gypsies."

"That comes to about six hundred thousand . . ."

"Add to that the two to three hundred thousand who had already been killed, and that makes more than eight hundred thousand."

"I would round up. Don't forget that they sometimes brought in as many as a thousand at a time."

Karl had been lying on his stomach, but now he turned over and surveyed the whole assembly site, the multicolored chaos of all those tattered blankets, the half-naked bodies with their shaved heads. "So this is what is left of a million people."

After morning roll call Küttner sends the camouflage commando to the lumberyard. We are supposed to take over the work of the woodcutters. They herd a few more people in. Robert is among them. As usual, guards, with rifles slung over their shoulders, are patrolling along the fence. Every once in a while they yell out to their comrades in the watchtower at this end of the camp. From time to time an SS man makes the rounds of the lumberyard, probably for no other reason than to carry out Kiewe's orders. He's thinking about the incident with the woodcutters. Many of the SS are now on leave. And it is very hot. The ground, the grass, and the trees are parched, and not even the morning brings relief. As the afternoon progresses and the temperature rises, fatigue settles over the camp. But it is masking an almost electric tension.

From up front, from the path along the SS barracks, we hear a distant clatter. It's the horse cart coming to pick up the trash that's been collected by the cleaning crew. The clatter has stopped, and suddenly our saw is sticking. Now the cart is in front of the entrance, right next to the munitions depot. They're loading the garbage, and this time they've got the triggers too. "Men, I beg you, do something, get moving, pull on that saw. You can't just stand around like this!" Kleinmann is running around getting us to work, and we don't notice the cart pull away.

After a while we get the news that the nest has been taken out. Lublink is our contact, and he's working somewhere near the intersection between the ghetto, the SS barracks, and Ukrainian barracks. Messages and instructions are being carried by whomever Kleinmann sends out, supposedly to go to the latrines.

The crowd at the kitchen is not as large as usual. Standing in line, I can see that some of the men are squeezing their hands. I recall a scene in the small town where my grandfather used to live. It's Yom Kippur, and Jews from the surrounding countryside all come into town and greet each other with handshakes, wishing each other well . . . They have come from all the small villages and gathered for this holiday—this day of reconciliation.

In spite of the heat we carry our bowls into the barracks to our bunks. We want to see Rudi and talk to him. "Two cases have already been distributed. That's thirty pieces—down in the workshops—in the latrine—in the pigeon house. What would the Doll Franz have to say about that? And there are five rifles—only five rifles—Kurland's got a pistol in the upper camp—and some bottles filled with gasoline." Rudi is no longer capable of putting together an entire sentence. Nor is anyone else. "Boys—if one of you—tell the ones at home, the ones out there . . ."

Rudi takes each of us by the hand, one after the other, but Hans refuses: "Wait until this evening, when it's all called off again . . ."

David's thin face appears below. He has come to take his leave. A singing, rhythmic monotone can be heard coming from the opposite bunk, a voice that rises above the din. David grabs me by the arm: "Do you hear that? King David's Psalm: 'Yea, though I walk through the valley of the shadow of death, I will fear no evil, for Thou art with me . . .'"

Robert is sitting on his folded blankets, tired. His elbows resting on his knees, he turns his head from side to side in order to survey the entire scene.

"Today we are Treblinka . . ." The work crews are marching out to work again after their midday break, and they're singing the Treblinka song.

Kleinmann uses the return to work as an opportunity to pass on information. From the outside it looks as if he's giving instructions for work: "Things start at precisely four o'clock. We are responsible for our guard here, for the one along the fence, and the one at the gate, and of course for any SS man who might happen along this way. Rifles and anything else that shoots are to be handed over immediately to Josek and Herschek. They know how to use them; they have served in the military. We have no weapons other than those we take off of them. There might be another bottle or two of gasoline for the lumberyard here. We must set everything on fire, immediately. We will keep to this side of the Ukrainian barracks." Kleinmann looks around in the direction of the watchtower beyond the green fence: "Well, it is quite a ways from there to here, but we can never let them completely out of our sight."

The camouflage commando gets back to work in the lumberyard, cutting branches, chopping and splitting logs. Karl and I pick up our saw again. Suchomel is the only boss at the site. In his white summer uniform, he's riding around on a bicycle. There is not a cloud in the sky—only bright blue sky as far as the eye can see—and the sun is beating down mercilessly, silencing everyone and making it difficult to breathe.

"Kleinmann, what time is it?"

"Almost two."

"Is your watch right?"

From way in the front, near the fork in the path, in the direction of the headquarters building, Lublink gives a signal with his raised arm, all the while looking as if he were simply wiping his sweaty face on his sleeve. Kleinmann subtly turns toward Lublink and then returns somewhat more quickly, but still in a very measured gait: "Listen, from now on we go the moment they make the slightest move to take anyone off to the infirmary or threaten to kill. Not one more man is going to die that way."

This means that the gasoline bottles have also been distributed. How many will David Brat have hidden up in Barracks A? He stayed back there with five or six people to clean up. Down here we still don't have a single bottle. On the other side of the Ukrainian barracks, spread out over the site, the potato commando buried a few bottles instead of potatoes. We had enough bottles in camp. But paper and matches were always in short supply in Treblinka.

"You," Kleinmann turned toward me, "go up to the barracks with some lumber and other supplies. Act as if you're looking for another saw, and on the way, tell Lublink and the others that things are still under control down here." I take the path along the Ukrainian barracks, passing by the Zoo Corner. Beda waves at me. He is the one who fixed up the zoo like this. He put in a garden around the periphery. He covered the paths with sifted yellow sand, not with the ashen gray earth from over there. He covered the roof and the pillars with split white birch. He enclosed the entire garden with low birch fencing, and he edged the lawn with bright-colored gravel. Beda is only eighteen years old. He comes from the countryside somewhere near Prague and was trained as a gardener. His mother, as was common, had a little shop in the village. He didn't have a father. When we arrived in Treblinka, we got off the train together and helped each other to carry our luggage to the disrobing site—him, me, and his *maminka*, his mother.

A nod is enough for Lublink to understand that everything's okay. Rudi must already have emptied the pigeon houses that stand at the fork in the path leading in one direction to the ghetto, and in the other to the SS barracks. He's probably carrying the hand grenades with him.

"Ah, ah, where are you going, and what do you want?" Mietek asks as I am about to cross the assembly site and continue on to the upper camp.

"To say that everything's okay down where we are—and I'm supposed to go up to the disrobing site, too."

"Ah, I see," he says, pointing behind him: "I can't let anyone into the latrine now. They're preparing a few gifts for *das Simches Tojre*— the Torah Festival."

I step out onto the empty square in front of the train station. Suddenly, under the blinding sun, I am again overcome by that strange feeling. From up here I look down on this entire scene and seem not to be a part of it. I am nothing but an astounded, fascinated observer.

It is not the same place it was ten months ago. A white sign with large black letters informs arriving passengers that this place is called "Treblinka—Obermajdan." There are smaller signs mounted below to guide them on their way: "Trains to Białystok and Wolkowisk," "To the Baths." Other signs can be found over the blind windows of Barracks A, on this side of the platform: "Tickets," "Arrivals." Up on the gable there is an oversized clock face. Its hands always show six o'clock. Before you get to the disrobing site, on the back wall of the garage, you will see a fake door marked "Stationmaster." The clear varnish coating on the walls of Barracks B makes it shimmer in the sun. A sign indicates that freight is handled there. The narrow strips of grass along the barracks are supposed to have a soothing effect on passersby. The deep rich green of the fence contrasts with the bright pastel green of the grassy embankment. Leading over the two shiny, well-traveled rails, there is a broad, bright white crossing. The surface of the platform and of the entire train station is a cindery black. The building blocks of Treblinka consist of a wild mix of forms and colors. Hanging over the main gate is a carved wooden globe with a compass. The SS insignia cuts across it. The guardhouse is decorated with carvings. The wood-carvers were taken off the transports.

Everything was taken away from them except their craft, their art.

And you can probably imagine what the headquarters looks like! The gray of asphalt lanes is enclosed with a border of matt-white limestone. The shimmering yellow of sand-covered walks and pathways is edged with beds of multicolored stone—a kaleidoscope. At every corner you will find signs decorated with carvings. Under the words "To the Ghetto," there is the bent figure of a Jew carrying a bundle on his back. The sign on the main street is decorated with two SS figures, and the inscription indicates that this Treblinka boulevard is named after the oldest member of the local SS special commando: "Karl-Seidel-Straße." The next sign, "Max-Biala-Kaserne," directs us to the barracks that house the Ukrainian guards.

In passing, I cautiously look toward the garage. "Standa?" From the depths of the building he steps out into the light, wiping his oil-smeared hands with a rag. "Everything's good." A tin drum has been rolled out to the garage entrance and braced with a rock. Next to it there are several containers. All that needs to be done is to open them and let the contents trickle out over the forty to fifty meters of cinders to the large gas tank. From there it is less than twenty meters to the closest SS barracks.

After I get back and report to Kleinmann, Karl and I start sawing again. "Kleinmann, what time . . . ?"

"Almost three: two fifty-seven. Be careful. Kiewe is on a rampage again. He's already administered one beating, and he took down someone else's number. That'll be twenty-five lashes at evening roll call."

"*Jach, hab' große Mojre*—I'm afraid he's not going to get his twenty-five."

Adjacent to the lumberyard there is a grass-covered plot fenced with nothing but chicken wire. The laundry for the SS and the Ukrainian guards is hung out here to bleach and to dry. Three girls are just now approaching with their baskets to take in the dry wash. They stretch up to reach the clothesline. I recalled scenes like this from home: women in their light sleeveless blouses reaching for clothespins, their skirts hitching up.

I look over to the watchtower. "Hey, Kleinmann, what's with the watchtower? Who's got it?"

"Not us, and it almost looks as if no one's got it. That'd be insane.

The way it stands now, they can get a real good shot at anyone who's running. We're going to have to be damned fast . . ."

"How much longer?"

"Twelve minutes."

"Hmm, almost closing time."

Suchomel pedals around our group a couple of times and then rides away on a path along the fence in the direction of the main thoroughfare. "He's on his break, going to have a little drink of coffee." Josek watches him as he rides off. "He could've stayed here a little longer."

"Five minutes. Well, I guess I'll get back up to the front again." Kleinmann disappears behind us.

Someone comes running through the trees at the same time Kleinmann races up to us: "Kiewe's caught somebody. It looks as if they might be taking him to the infirmary. Kuba, the barracks elder, had just reported something to him." Everyone stops. No one says a word. With both hands Foreman Kleinmann reaches under his glasses to wipe away the perspiration, and then he looks at his watch: "Two minutes to four."

It's the second of August, nineteen hundred and forty-three.

Out front, somewhere in the vicinity of our living quarters, a shot rings out. Afterward silence. Then the first hand grenade explodes, followed immediately by the second. I see the third one detonate on the asphalt lane. We no longer see the guard who had been behind us, and the one at the gate has disappeared as well. Josek and Herschek have their weapons: "Revolution! The end of the war!" The second part of the slogan is meant to confuse the guards.

"Hurrah!" You hear it here and there, timidly at first. It sticks in my chest and catches in my throat until I can finally scream: "Hurrah!" The yelling gets louder and rises over the entire Treblinka complex. Something flies through the air over my head and explodes in front of the Ukrainian barracks. The dry twigs and the pine branches catch fire instantly. Flames shoot up everywhere. The gate to Camp 2 is wide open, and a figure with a rifle is kneeling on the other side. Judging by the round, shaved head, it might be Zelo. "Kiewe's got his," I hear a voice yell.

Among the trees, racing out from the SS barracks, a figure appears in a white shirt, without a jacket, and then suddenly disappears behind an exploding grenade. More flames leap into the air, and now the Ukrainian barracks are beginning to burn. All of a sudden, his arms spread wide, Robert falls onto a pile of chopped branches, the way boys throw themselves into a mound of hay, and he doesn't move. Saul is at the very front. Karl is running in front of me, to my left, swinging his spade over his head, and then he stops. Somehow he just can't keep going. Beyond the tree, near the barracks, I can see the chief guard, Rogoza, shooting in the direction of the lumberyard. Why am I carrying this ax, anyway?

Coming from up front, somewhere near the intersection at the SS barracks, we hear a long, drumfire barrage. Who got there first, Rudi or them? A quick hissing sound, and the subsequent explosion blinds me, everything quakes under my feet, the pine tree in front of the kitchen bursts into black-bordered flames. I hear a weaker but constant crackling and see fire breaking out everywhere. So he did it. Standa Lichtblau . . .

We duck and somehow reach the yard in front of the Ukrainian barracks. There are only a few of us. At a loss, Josek is standing there with his empty rifle in his hands. Herschek is nowhere to be seen.

Lublink is running along the barracks carrying some kind of pole in his hand and chasing people out in front of him like a gooseherd, pointing to the back gate, which leads out onto the field surrounding the camp: "Outta here, everyone outta here—into the woods!" The gate is broken down. We run out and on across the vegetable field.

"Karl, hey Karl!" We're both laughing like mad, running next to each other. I scream, and I hear myself continuing to scream in wild celebration. I run up the front of a pile of manure and leap off the other side. Something whistles through the air around me. You idiot, can't you keep under cover—they're whistling in from both sides, from the watchtowers no one got. Dust swirls up out of the parched vegetable field.

Then all of a sudden, there's barbed wire in front of us, strung diagonally between the tank traps. There are already a lot of us on the ground, falling down, falling back and moaning. Slowly, like setting your feet down on a rope, just not too fast now, yea-h-h. Karl had already jumped through in front of me. We start running again. "Where now?"

"Everyone on our right is headed into the woods!"

"No, we're better off on the left. Over there into the peat bogs!"

Now there are only three of us. The dark-complected Schlojme, another one from camouflage, is running in front of us. Suddenly there's a small pond before us. Leaping through the bushes on the shore, directly into the water, we quickly reach the middle. Out in front of us Schlojme is already approaching the opposite side when a black uniform appears. A shot, a scream. I dive under the surface, and half swimming, half crawling along the muddy bottom, I return to the other shore where we jumped in. There I find a thicket of branches growing out into the water. Shots whip the surface of the water around me and over me. When I reach the shore I take a quick breath and immediately dive under the surface again. Someone grabs at me: Karl wants to make sure I'm still here.

After a few moments of silence and quick breaths, I take a chance and hold my head above the surface again. Standing next to me, Karl is also looking around. We find ourselves at twilight completely hidden behind a dense curtain of willow branches. At our backs is a muddy embankment so high and so soft that we can firmly sit ourselves into it. "Thought we'd had it." We communicate more with our eyes than with our mouths. "We'll have to wait here until it's completely dark." Holding our mouths just at the surface of the water, we carefully dig out the bank behind us with our fingers. We cannot allow even the tiniest ripple to spread from under the overhanging branches.

In the distance, from Treblinka, we hear a rumbling, probably an armored vehicle, and then shots. The water is warm, "like coffee," we'd say at home. We really have chosen the right time to go swimming. The sun is shimmering through the branches, and a dragonfly flits gracefully over the water.

There's a roar from the road, from Malkinia, then right above us as if the motor were suspended directly over our heads. A reconnaissance plane? We're surrounded by voices, yelling, screaming, and then interrupted by shots. The sound of barking dogs cuts through the din of human voices. The voices and the barking come closer—closer and closer—now, now they're here, right over us—now—no, now they're going away, farther away. Silence. More noise—from the opposite shore—some kind of vehicle—it sounds as if they're loading up the dead.

By the time the sun touches the horizon we hear nothing but the quiet noises made by insects, and the buzzing grows louder as the last rays of the sun disappear. Mosquitoes land on our faces. The more often we dip our faces into the water, the larger the swarms sucking our blood become. The skin on my forehead is so tightly drawn that it feels as though it's going to split, and I sense that my eyes and my cheeks are beginning to swell . . . As time passes the water is getting colder. No, it's just as warm as it was, but we've been soaking for six hours. Trembling has given way to chills. Our knees are knocking together under the water.

By the time we reach the other shore and wade out, in complete darkness, the sky behind us is beginning to get lighter, and as we crawl up on the shore and turn around, we see an immense fire over Treblinka, larger and of a different color than on all those previous nights when the flames had been fed by the large incineration grates.

On through Poland:

A Little to the Left, and Then to the Right

I am awakened by the sun lying low on the horizon. I have slept through the entire day. And with this clear blue sky, it must have been just as scorchingly hot as it was yesterday. I am lying in some bushes, comfortably bedded down in the mown straw we gathered from a nearby field this morning. Karl is still asleep next to me. He is barefoot and covered with dried blood, scratches, and mud, and I'm sure I look like that too. If we went in the right direction during the night, then we should already be a few kilometers away from Treblinka.

As we climbed out onto the shore under cover of darkness and saw Treblinka in flames behind us, all sensation of tiredness and cold simply dropped away. We had to get away, away from those roaring flames. Again and again we sank down into the peat bog, pulled each other out and sank, all the while stifling the urge to break out in insane laughter.

It wasn't until we had left the Bug River far behind us that we finally stopped. By night we will try to make our way through Poland to the Slovakian border and on into the Beskid Mountains. Maybe we can hide out there, and maybe we'll find other fugitives or resistance groups. So we should keep heading in a southwesterly direction. We'll have to orient ourselves by the North Star, Ursa Minor, Ursa Major, and the flames of Treblinka. Following guidelines in the sky, we'll have to flee along the ground through swamps, underbrush, and forests and across fields of tall unmown grain. We'll stop from time to time, look up to the stars, and reckon: "Look there, shouldn't we be going a little more to the right and then a little to the left?" Behind us the flames grow smaller and fade. By dusk they have become gray.

Karl is waking up. He raises his head and blinks at me: "Well, no roll call today. How cautious will they be when they report to their superiors about what has happened in Treblinka? Maybe they'll all be punished for having let things come to this end."

"Or maybe they'll just try to cover it all up, the whole barbarous mess. And that'll mean that as soon as we get a little farther away from Treblinka, nobody will know a thing about it. There won't be any reports."

"Maybe all they'll do is send out a few special search units."

"Maybe not even that. How will anyone really know how many of us were caught and finished off, or how many of us really got away? I'd be willing to bet that our SS boys will report that they got us all, not a single witness running around on the outside, everything's under control."

"That means . . . ?"

"And who are we anyway, who are we claiming to be?"

"I couldn't tell you now. All I know is that tonight we've got a lot of ground to cover, and then maybe we'll think of something." Karl looks at his bare feet. His boots had come off in the muddy bottom of the lake when we were under fire. We hadn't been able to find them again in the dark. So Karl declared right then and there that he would cross the whole damned country of Poland barefoot.

"From what I have seen of these things in the movies, I don't think our little uprising was all that exemplary. Sure, we threw a few hand grenades into the air and set everything on fire. But after that we just fumbled around and let ourselves be shot at like fish in a barrel."

"Standa Lichtblau probably accomplished the most by blowing up the gas tank."

"Always said he wouldn't leave his wife and child behind, on the other side. All the older ones who had come with their families said that. And they organized the whole thing."

"I'll tell you, they were so single-minded, they never intended to escape themselves. They just wanted us younger ones to get out. There's no other way to explain why Lublink herded us out through the fence the way he did . . ."

"And I never saw him after that."

"So Galewski and the ones around him—Kurland, Sudowicz, Simcha the carpenter—they had no intention of escaping?"

"And what about our Rudi?"

"He had family on the other side. Always talked about how she had been pregnant and how much he loved her."

"Always acted like he was something better, all that fine talk . . . and then he showed us all what kind of a man he is—was."

"Hans Freund, on the other hand, had given up before we even got started. He never believed we'd pull it off . . ."

"Maybe it was his family, they were on the other side too."

"But Robert Altschul, it wasn't his mind, it was his body that gave in. He just couldn't hold out, he was too weak."

And the guards, they never stopped boozing and stuffing their faces, they fought for every *Hrosche*—every penny. But they must have had orders about how to handle an outbreak like this. You could tell by the way some of them raced to the outside and surrounded the camp.

Karl tears off several heads from the grain stalks he has been sleeping on, rubs them between his hands, blows away the awn and the chaff, leaving only the kernels behind. He shakes a few of them into his mouth and then offers the rest to me: "Look, this is a good sign. How do believers put it: the hand of the Lord is opened?"

As the sun begins to set, but still in daylight, we leave our hideout in order to orient ourselves before it gets too dark. An endlessly wide plain spreads out before us. On the horizon beyond, we can see a weighted wooden beam rising into the sky, and we assume that it must be part of a well tower. The little house next to it seems to be alone on this flat piece of the world. It lures us like a vision, even though we know it may also mean danger. Will we ever reach it? We have been running from one stand of bushes to another for so long, and the well-water gallows is still so far off in the distance. But when the little house finally begins to grow larger, we can see signs of life. A woman in a head scarf, her back bent, is approaching the well.

We have to try, we have to ask, but from a distance. We don't know who else might be in the hut. Even the old woman might be dangerous. Anyone we meet may be an enemy. Her face turned toward us, the old woman stops, but she doesn't really seem all that surprised to see us. "Well, going to Warsaw, to the Vistula? This is Ostrów. You should be going the other way, over there. It'd be best just to keep following the road." She stands up a little straighter and looks us over more carefully: "*Uciekacie z niewoly, tak?*—You're escaping prisoners of war, aren't you? But you're not Poles . . ."

"*Tak, tak*—yes, yes," we nod. "*My Czechy*—from prison camp, we're Czechs . . ."

We disappear into the twilight behind the next stand of bushes and repeat the magic formula that the old woman unwittingly set on our tongues. "Hey, now do you know who we are and what we're doing? We're Czechs, and we're escaping from a prisoner of war camp. She must have seen lots of prisoners of war passing by here— Poles, maybe a Russian or two, a Ukrainian. Why not a few Czechs too? Yes, we're Czechs, and we want to get back home, somewhere off to the southwest."

First past Warsaw and over the Vistula. We can both remember at least that much of our geography lessons. But we're complete failures when it comes to navigating by the stars. Our Boy Scout skills have left us in the lurch, but not our luck—not yet, anyway. Up to this point we have actually been heading toward the Russian front. And this is probably our great good fortune, since the Germans will hardly have thought of sending a search party off in this direction. What a marvelous blunder.

Things that seem simple by twilight, when you can easily see the road to Warsaw leading off between rows of trees, become difficult by night. From time to time we even have to walk along the shoulder of the road in order not to lose our way. In complete darkness we bump into each other, and we practically have our noses in the signs before we can spell out the names of towns and villages—Wyszków, Radzymin. How many nights have we been walking since we escaped Treblinka? We don't know anymore. We begin to see signs of a more densely populated area: beams of light that cut through the darkness, fences, and barking dogs.

On one of these nights a command rings out from the direction of the road: "Halt!" We run away and hide in a potato field, lying motionless for hours. It looks as if we'll have to give up walking so close to the road, since there are houses everywhere. We're going to have to risk traveling by daylight, at least for a while, so that we can avoid settlements. It's okay. We even have the feeling that this has become less dangerous than moving at night. Each day we leave our hiding place a little earlier. Grazing cows, like guideposts, let us know which direction we should be taking. From the other side we are protected by long rows of bushes that are supposedly here to keep the wind from scalping the low-growing vegetation off these flat fields.

By the light of day we can seek out an isolated hut and wait for the appropriate time to ask for a little something to eat. The magic formula "We are Czechs, escaping prisoners of war," continues to work. And in these situations it is better to speak only Czech. It seems strange, but because it is a Slavic language we can make ourselves understood.

"Don't worry. Now, during the war years, we see so many people passing through—Poles, Russians, and whoever else. Our feelings tell us to feed a hungry man and ask no questions. Your good sense tells you to eat your fill and then continue on your way." These are the words a peasant woman used to reassure us.

One day we are following a path that intersects so abruptly with a small village lane that we cannot avoid a group of people walking our way. Among them are two German soldiers in uniform. Nothing happens. We walk right past them, and no one pays us any attention. Of course, by now we look exactly like the ragged speculators of the region—both of us barefoot, one of us with dry muddy boots slung over his shoulder, our pants torn practically to shreds. It is impossible to tell what color our crumpled shirts and jackets once were. With a new sense of self-assurance, we simply walk along the sidewalks past houses big and small, continuing on our way. From road signs we read the names of places we have never heard of before—Rembertów, Solejuwky.

We head in the direction in which civilization is rapidly thinning out and heave a sigh of relief once we again find ourselves moving freely through open land. We even dare to approach three peasants who are raking straw in a small field. "You want to get to the Vistula, without going through Warsaw? It won't be easy. The German military is everywhere. They're on patrol, keeping watch." The man, with a weathered face and nothing more than a vest covering his bare torso, turns to talk to the woman and the girl. He turns back to us: "The only thing you can do is cross through the old army shooting range. From time to time they test a few weapons or explosives. Otherwise no one dares to go anywhere near there. If you get through, you can go straight on through the forest and across the road to the Vistula."

We crawl under the barbed wire and out onto a field that is somehow less dangerous for us because it is so dangerous for everyone else. Black grass, black earth—everything is burned.

As we crawl out again from under strands of barbed wire, from the blackened enclosure and into the living forest, we can already see the road among the trees. On the edge of a small clearing that drops off directly onto the road, we stop and look around. We see the top of a man's back in a pit. We could ask this man how to get to the Vistula from here. We step out into the light. Green uniforms appear on the road at a point just beyond the edge of the forest— German military police on horseback. The very next moment, and for as long as it took for the Germans to ride by and disappear into the forest again, there were three ragged men digging and shoveling in the pit, their heads under caps with worn and crumpled visors. Two of them are muttering through clenched teeth: "Keep digging. Keep on. One word, one false move, and you'll feel it right here in your skull . . ."

Karl has the ax in his hand. I've got the shovel that the man had left on the edge of the pit while he was continuing to dig with a pickax. Once more, something had clicked in our heads as we each jumped into the pit without hesitation and started digging.

Now that the danger has passed, we seem to be more agitated than this man. When we explain apologetically that we are "escaping prisoners of war," he just waves us off, saying he has gotten used to so many *wypadki*—so many unexpected events. Then he shows us where to go. A short way beyond the road we discover a barn that is some distance from an isolated farmhouse. At dusk we lie down in a ditch, where we have a good view of the barn, and wait until it is dark. Karl lifts me up, and I wriggle in over the top of the door. From inside the barn, I unlock the door and let Karl in. The barn must already be rather full. In the dark it smells of grain and straw, and coming from somewhere up in the rafters is the fragrance of hay. We follow our noses into the haymow and simply let ourselves drop in exhaustion.

After the first few moments of rest, hunger takes over. The last time we had anything to eat was sometime yesterday. We burrow more deeply into the hay in order to keep warm. Next to me Karl is becoming restless: "Hey, I can feel something hard down here."

"Down here, something hard? Maybe someone left a pitchfork." Karl feels around, and then he shoves something into my face—an apple. Apples are stored in the hay right where we lay down. Is all this good fortune a sign of our fate, is the hand of the Lord going to stay open, or both, and everything together? The next day, as we drag ourselves down to the Vistula, our stomachs ache from all those apples.

On one of the many piles at the sorting site in Treblinka I found a tiny leather case that contained a complete shaving kit. It was so small that I could easily slip it into my pocket. Its owner must have been a very practical man to have packed something like that for the transport. Ever since coming across it I have kept the little case with me. Now we are standing naked in the water at a bend in the river and shaving. What I see reflected in the Vistula only dimly resembles what I remember of my face.

The little kit has much more than just a practical value for us. There are four small diamonds embedded in the round piece of shaving soap. We got them from Willy Fürst and Salo Sauer, two of the Gold Jews, on the night before the uprising, just in case . . . Karl and I had made an agreement: If we were to survive, it would be without the help of these diamonds. We would never use them for any purpose other than as mementos.

Piaseczno, Góra Kalwaria, Grójec, Mogielnica—those are the exotic-sounding names of towns we passed through, more or less without incident. Beyond the river, which, as we later learn, is called the Pilica, we again find ourselves in the forest, the place we feel most secure.

"Halt, rence do gory—hands over your heads!" we hear a voice ring out among the trees. Our heads bowed and our hands raised, we are looking into the muzzle of a rifle. The man behind it looks like both a forester and a customs agent. He is mixing Polish and German: "Who are you, what are you doing here?"

"We're Czechs. We came to Poland in the German Todt Organization. Somewhere in the woods, on the other side of the Vistula, we were attacked by partisans, robbed, and beaten. We've been on the run for several days now, and we don't know where to go or what to do. The uprising must have spread everywhere. We want to go home to Czechoslovakia."

"You can tell your story to the police in town. There isn't any uprising around here, but there are a lot of bandits wandering around. Not a step closer, just turn around and march!" This fellow in his forester's getup, his finger on the trigger the whole time, is acting as if partisans and bandits might come storming out of the forest at any moment—but not a one appeared . . .

"We'll use the names we agreed on," Karl whispers to me along the way. I want to tell him that he's crazy, that other names would be a lot better. But I can't. We can't get into any lengthy discussion right under our captor's eyes. The story about the Todt Organization, and the Czechs who had been attacked by the partisans, was something we had picked up and put together from what we had been told by the people we had met in the huts and fields. It had occurred to Karl that he could use the name of a friend of his from Olmütz: he would be Vladimir Frysak. Karl had heard that Frysak was supposedly doing forced labor somewhere in Germany or Austria. So assuming they didn't check things out too carefully back home . . . I had been thinking of using the name Rudolf Masarek. I know his address in Prague. And as far as I know, he had not been registered as a Jew—until he got married. "We're just going to have to keep repeating these names to ourselves until we go nuts," Karl mumbles.

Nowe Miasto nad Pilicą, "New Town on the Pilica," where the watchful forester is taking us, is a village that we had already spotted from a distance. He takes us straight across the bumpy village square, only partially paved, to the police station. We see nothing but Polish uniforms here, no German ones yet. We are relieved and encouraged. We repeat the story about Czechs in German labor commandos who were attacked by the partisans. It looks as if the policemen are not entirely unwilling to believe what we've been saying. We sense some reluctance, especially because we are Czechs, and we speak Czech. It's an unusual and somewhat confusing case.

"We want to go back home to Czechoslovakia," we say, and when we see that this has had the desired effect, we are emboldened. "We'll lodge a complaint with our government."

"Yes, with our government!" Karl says with such conviction that even I have begun to believe it.

They are almost apologetic as they put us in handcuffs. They have an amusing name for handcuffs in Polish: *kajdanki*. "We don't have a choice. There are bandits and vagrants everywhere. We're going to transfer you . . ." They never use the word *partisan*. And they won't tell us where we're to be transferred either. It wouldn't be wise to ask too many questions.

The street, which begins at one corner of the village square and runs past small houses and huts, appears to lead into a void. From there, along the entire length of what is basically an unpaved street, the setting sun shines until its last rays have been extinguished. Its light flares up once more, reflecting off the handcuffs, which emphasize our vagrancy. Behind us strides a policeman whose only indication of rank is the cap on top of his head. Other than that he's dressed in street clothes. Here and there we see people standing in doorways and staring. One of the men, barefoot, wearing a shirt, his hands in his pockets, yells in our direction: "Hey, Wujtek, got a couple of Jews to shoot?"

Out of the corner of my eye I see the policeman's cap shaking a negative response. Then I hear the voice: "Probably some kind of bandits."

"Well, all right, so we're bandits. At least we're not . . ." we mumble and stop short of saying the word.

The policeman locks us up in a dark hole at the edge of the village. After a short time we sense that we're not alone on the damp, hardened floor. Some human creature, apparently shot in one leg, is crying and moaning the entire night, prophesying in Polish: "We're all going to get a bullet in the head, right through the skull . . ."

The next morning they march us back along the same street to the police station, where a wagon and horse are waiting. They put us in the middle. The man who was wearing a cap yesterday, and today has added a jacket, sits with his rifle pointing to the front. The man in full uniform sits at the back with his rifle over his knees, positioning himself to keep an eye on us.

Before leaving the village we stop at a small house. It probably belongs to one of the policemen. We are allowed to get down off the wagon. When two or three women see that the three of us, bound together by our handcuffs, have carefully bent over in unison to harvest the windfall, they shake the trees until more apples and pears fall into the wagon. And before we have even left the village behind, our starving stomachs are attempting to come to terms with a heavy, aching bounty.

On this lovely late summer's day, our coach, actually nothing more than a narrow pallet with wheels, bumps along through Polish orchards on the banks of the Pilica river. From time to time it has to stop. We two vagrants jump down and hop quickly to the edge of the road. There, in a ditch, one of us takes his pants down and goes into a crouch, holding his handcuffed hand in the air, while the other bends over slightly, stretching his handcuffed hand out to his partner. Positions are traded several times.

The two policemen are rather considerate, even if they never put down their guns. There is only one longer stretch through the forest where the one in the back yells to the one in the front: "*Teraz uwaga*—let's watch out here." They hold their rifles at the ready. They don't stop. Apparently there is a chance that the partisans may interrupt us while we are taking a shit—but they don't . . .

In the meantime we are fiercely determined to keep up this crazy act of "the poor, lost Czechs." Any attempt to flee would mean giving up this front. And anyway, how could we escape when we are attached to each other with these *kajdanki*? So we go over every detail of our stories again and again. We confirm addresses and birthdates. We question each other as if we were conducting a hearing.

We come upon a sign that reads "Tomaszów Mazowiecki." There are small squat huts crowded closely together, giving way to multi-storied buildings as our coach begins to rumble over paved streets. This town is too big. There may even be a Gestapo post here. If they turn us over it'll be the end, the bitter end . . .

The reception room looks like a gatehouse, and people here are speaking both Polish and German. No Gestapo, no exacting discipline. We are reassured. We speak more loudly than the quasi-civilians who are walking around with pistols and keys hanging from their belts. We speak even more loudly when we speak Czech, because there's not really any other language we can safely use to communicate with each other.

"For the time being" we're put downstairs in the cellar, in a room with such a low ceiling that we must either lie down or sit hunched over on the floor. After three days in this hole I am suddenly overcome with the need to scream: "'Crucified on my back—soaked through—for what?'" But Karl, who is lying next to me, would just call me an asshole . . . Contrary to our expectations, the first hearing, which takes place after a few days' stay in the cellar, is not all that thorough. We are used to other sorts of questioning, and furthermore we are no longer just playing our roles. We are living them; we have climbed into them. We believe what we are saying.

Bandits, partisans, attacked us. The entire work crew was scattered. We had been working on the edge of the forest in some kind of fortification not far from Wyszków, or some little town with a name like that. We had only been there for three days, living in small cabins, near a convent . . . The part about the convent was true. The nuns there gave us food after we escaped Treblinka.

"When officials from the Protectorate of Bohemia and Moravia sent us there, we could not have imagined, even in our worst dreams, what we were getting into . . ." As I am saying this, slipping into colloquial Czech which they hardly understand at all, I sense some bitterness. These quasi-civilians, who speak half Polish and half German, are *Volksdeutsche*—the Polish Germans, or German Poles, Lublink and David Brat had told us about in Treblinka. They won't likely know very much about the Protectorate of Bohemia and Moravia. Just be careful, if they start screaming or taking a swing at us—there's a whip hanging on the wall. We're going to have to be quicker, start yelling before they do, louder, bang on the tables. Still, they've got to recognize that what they see here is a couple of men who've been driven to the edge by what's been happening to them, not just a couple of fakes.

Our unusual case remains undecided, and we are led to an upstairs cell. This is not a real prison cell. Both the walls and the beds are nailed together from pieces of lumber. There are so many people here that we have to sleep in shifts. Some lie down on the pallets, which are lined up along the entire length of the wall and take up about four-fifths of the available space. The others doze, leaning up against the opposite wall, in a passageway so narrow that two people can hardly pass by one another.

After a few days in this transitional pen we begin to get a more complete picture of our situation. These wooden cells were built into what was once a Jewish-owned factory, and here the bedbugs thrive, reproduce, and suck themselves full of our blood, a continuous torment for us all. This is a consolidated prison, where they lock up everyone together, no matter what they've done—suspected "partisans and bandits," as well as thieves, crooks, black marketeers, and all sorts of strange and shady characters.

The dried-up German lying in the most privileged position, on a pallet in front of the door, keeps telling us that Salvarsan is the only thing that will help him. He never stops talking about this medication. Maybe he's practicing his role as a syphilitic, talking to himself, getting inside it. The handsome blond man, named Leon Dubel, is distinguished from all the rest of us in that he's wearing a dignified summer suit, light-colored pants and jacket, both striped. He's also wearing expensive brown oxfords, but without socks, simply shoes on his bare feet. The socks were supposedly left behind when he suddenly had to interrupt a liaison with his boss's wife. But maybe this elegant man is really a contact for the resistance, and this story about the woman is just a front.

The little farmer stretched out in the middle of the line is a black marketeer dealing in meat, lard, and suet. With his deeply pious mien, he claims that these things were mainly intended for the production of candles. He's the only one in the cell with special permission to supplement his jailhouse diet with delicacies from home. Every morning, while the rest of us are slurping down the usual chicory brew from our tin bowls, the little farmer kneels down in front of a pallet, leans on his elbows, folds his hands, and prays facing the wall, the same way he does at home, where he has hung the portrait of a saint. Here in the cell, the only things hanging on the wall are the bloody remains of squashed bedbugs. Once his morning prayers are finished, he crosses himself and reaches under the pallet for the covered basket he stores there. Of course none of us receive a single crumb. And this is how he partakes of his blessed meals alone in the cell.

Always, after a certain number of days, the door to the cell is opened in the early afternoon, and a boy of about thirteen is shoved under the bar and into our midst. Then we know it is Saturday. The boy had stolen a chair, and since he has to attend school during the week, he comes here on Saturdays and Sundays to serve out his fourteen-day sentence. He is our living calendar; with his help we count the weeks.

This pen is set up for transition and transfer, and with very few exceptions, when they let someone out, there are only two possible destinations. If they give you a pink form to sign after your hearing, it means you're on your way to Oświęcim, Auschwitz in German—never heard that name before. That's when motors start rumbling in the courtyard, spotlights shine, names are called, and people from the cells are loaded onto trucks. If, on the other hand, you are given a white form to sign, then it's off to Germany to work for the Reich. In this case, you are escorted to the train station in broad daylight.

This second option, going to work in Germany, seems so promising that we even pass up a good opportunity for escape. They are looking for assistant bricklayers. We volunteer, and the guard takes us somewhere to a site on the edge of town. "What was here before, what kind of buildings were these?"

"Ghetto, Jews—everyone sent away somewhere, everything torn down . . ."

Not a single piece of a single wall was left standing. Everywhere we look there is nothing but rubble, sites full of wasted bricks and stones. We squat down in the middle of it all and knock pieces of mortar off the bricks so that they can be reused. Under an overcast sky the wind blows a few torn pieces of paper into the air. There is a salutation written long ago. *Pane szanowny*—Dear Mr. Wächter "sent away somewhere . . ." Now here we are, the two of us squatting down here, and we know where. We stare into the sky far beyond the orange-green flames. We hear the ancient words and the New Testament: "*Eli, Eli*—they've thrown us into the fire and the flames . . ."

The second hearing is more thorough—actually just longer—because, as we learn, this is the way it ought to be. We are asked trick questions. We continue to be suspected of somehow having connections with partisans and bandits. But this is precisely where we have no need to dissemble. "We want to go home. You've been holding us for several weeks, and you've had plenty of time to telephone or telegraph . . ."

"That's not the way things are done here. We don't have time." They probably don't even know how to go about making contact! "You're going to be sent to Germany to work." We are given white forms to sign.

Careful! No smiles. Keep up the struggle: "But we want to go home!"

"You cannot. We have our orders. You will be issued transport papers, in your names, for your journey into the Reich. Now we are taking you to an assembly camp in Czenstochau. You will be sent on from there, and what you do from that time on will be your own business. You will have to take responsibility for yourselves." Karl and I look at each other and nod, indicating that we'd resigned ourselves to this outcome since we seemed to have no other choice.

This is the first time either of us has signed his new name. For some time now it has seemed to me that these Polish-German gangsters have been acting a lot like the thugs in Treblinka as the end neared, wandering around, grumbling to themselves: "Shit, shit, all of it shit."

As is required, all of our belongings, including my little shaving kit, are returned to us. We ask the prison barber, who is to give us a shave before we leave, to lather us with our own good soap. "*To je bardzo dobre mydlo, nadzwyczajne*—yes, it certainly is very good soap, quite extraordinary . . .*"

The assembly camp in Czenstochau is a huge transfer point with the motto *"Nach Deutschland zur Arbeit,"* "To Germany to work." There are very, very many workers needed in every German land. There is a lot of speculation and trading to be done here through the barbed wire—dried-up old boots from Treblinka for shoestrings, for example. Karl and I have to have a physical along with everyone else. But since there are so many of us with shriveled-up foreskin, no one really checks to see if we've been circumcised.

For the trip, we get hold of a square loaf of army bread along with a carton of artificial honey, which does a wonderful job of gluing up a hungry stomach. We are taken in units to the train station and put into rail cars—passenger cars. We hardly settle into our seats before falling asleep. Everything going on around us is fogged by extreme weariness.

They say that this rather large city, which appears so flat through the train window, is Katowice. After some time, the train stops at a smaller station. We can't be far from the former Polish-Moravian border. Our armed guard from Czenstochau is taking the rest of our group to another train, telling us: "You two are going to continue on your own, through Moravia and Vienna to Mannheim, just as it says in your transport instructions. This is the only document you'll have. There are checkpoints everywhere. If you try to run you'll be caught, and you'll pay for it."

The guard hands over our transport instructions. The compartment door closes behind the shoulder with the rifle. No one is guarding us. We are alone. The destination and address are written on the transport instructions: "Mannheim—Heinrich Lanz, Inc."

❀

Rhineland Steel and Rhineland Wine

No one, nothing, keeps us from getting out and running off, from searching out people we can trust, testifying and bearing witness. Where we are now is only about twenty kilometers away from Olmütz, Karl's birthplace and hometown. Our heads hang down in exhaustion and come to rest on one another's shoulder from time to time. Quietly determined, we wake each other and deliberate in hushed tones: "Everything is too well ordered here, we won't be able to hold out, and this damned thing might last for a good long time. Everybody will recognize you because you'll be at home. If you so much as shrug your shoulders, they'll know what you're thinking. You will turn everyone you talk to into a fugitive, and you can just imagine what they'll do with those people. And anyway, who's going to believe what we say? People will think that we're two madmen. Who will hide us and feed us—and for how long? Where do they send poor ragged creatures like us? To Germany—nowhere else but Germany. Around here we'll just be too conspicuous. But right here in our hands we have this wonderful document, and it means that we have an official existence. The Rhine, it's a long way off. We've never been there before, and how many people will we meet from the camp at Czenstochau? So let's keep going . . ."

In a half-empty compartment we are sitting next to the sliding door. It opens, and a green uniform appears—pass control. "You must also have some kind of personal identification."

"We did, but all we were given for this journey were these transport instructions. We were told that the rest of our papers were being sent directly to the factory. Even when we were working for the Todt Organization the leader kept our papers." This not so young man in the green uniform looks us over again. It appears that we aren't the first derelicts to be transported into the Reich to work, even if our predecessors had their documents in better order than we have ours. But what more can he want anyway? All of the dates are here, the official stamp of the Office of Labor, complete with eagle and swastika, and lastly, the entry: "Ordered to work at the firm of Heinrich Lanz, Incorporated, Mannheim." And we're even sitting in the right train, traveling in the right direction.

At Vienna West we have to wait almost until evening for our connecting train. "Hey, look at that guy there in uniform. He's missing a hand."

"I see one without a leg, and look how neatly he's folded that pants leg."

"Look, that one over there in the little cart doesn't have any legs."

"And the man who's pushing him's only got one arm."

"There's another wheelchair. Wait a minute, there's a whole gang of 'em. One, two, three, eight Germans in uniform and only twelve arms and nine legs."

About two hours after leaving Vienna, once darkness has fallen, we are torn out of our sleep by a second inspection. It proceeds in much the same way as the first, except this time I am even more convinced myself that the rest of my papers are being sent separately. It would be unfair for anyone to start pushing us around now for not having a complete set of papers. Our eyes fall shut again.

Explosion—gasoline—Standa Lichtblau. No, I'm on the train for Mannheim, and things are exploding around me . . . "Air attack, bombing raid," is what I hear. The train stops, and from time to time it shakes slightly. After some time everything is quiet. From far away we can hear a long, uninterrupted whine. "Broken off," the bombing raid's been broken off, "all clear." I'm hearing these terms for the first time, such nice new words. Shortly after daybreak the train stops at a large station. We get out.

Mannheim-Ludwigshafen, twin cities on the middle reaches of the Rhine, an industrial region in southwest Germany. Machine tools, chemicals, electronics. And my dear geography professor only saw fit to give me a "good" on my graduation exam. What day is today, 24 September 1943?

It hasn't even been two months since we escaped from the other side . . . Not even two months, and it seems more like two years. What's going on here? Is this station waking up, is this city waking up, so gloomy on this dark morning? Is everything recovering from some kind of shock? Images appear that I had taken to be the ruins of old castles, and they are still covered with dust and mortar. Well, here's where the bombs fell—not very long ago—maybe even this past night. Destruction, earthquakes, catastrophes—hurray. This is our greatest good fortune, our best chance.

"The Heinrich Lanz factory? It's not very far, just over the pedestrian bridge, across the tracks and then down that street to the left." That's supposed to be a street or an alley? With the houses ripped out, it looks like a wounded mouth full of missing teeth. What was it that Bredow told Siedel up there in Barracks A? Hey, you won't recognize anything anymore. Entire streets are gone.

In the gatehouse are black uniforms, some with red braid. We've never seen these uniforms before, and even the terminology is new: *Werkschutz*—Factory Patrol. One of the officers puts on his glasses in order to read our transport instructions. Then he leads us past various buildings and shops where things are rumbling, hammering, roaring, squealing, and whirring. On the tracks an amusing little engine is pushing two large, regular-sized cars. In the courtyard in front of the main office building there is a cast-iron statue of a man with long sideburns, an old-fashioned coat with tails, and a vest with a watch chain. Of course, this must be old Mr. Lanz. "The founder, right?"

In the reception area most people are in civilian dress, but there are also some uniforms that we recognize—green, that's the police. At the desks in front of us it's all business. An argument between two workers from the shop floor is being resolved. At another desk a violation is being dealt with, and someone else is looking for a place to live. The people standing in front of us—faces, hands, and work clothes all smeared an oily black—let fall a few words of Polish, and the people next to them seem to be speaking Ukrainian. But from the desks a chopped, monosyllabic German breaks in: "Foreigners here only—not there. Hey, you foreigners too." Aha, here the police are the guards and overseers of these people.

This green gendarme or police uniform does not look particularly threatening. It is worn. Instead of wearing boots, these feet resting under the desk are in oxfords, and the legs sport leather leggings. We've got leggings just like them at home in the closet. They're supposedly from World War I.

It is difficult to understand what the seated man in the green uniform is saying to the man in street clothes. Apparently they're speaking the local dialect. But we get the gist of what he's saying, namely that he and his family have just lost the last little bit of roof over their heads during the bombing raid, their little house that they had all worked so hard for. In the meantime he picks up our transport instructions with his stiff fingers. He copies down the information onto small cards, files two away, and gives two to us. He hardly looks at us. "Here's your factory pass. Have your photos taken, attach them here, and come back to my desk so I can stamp them. You'll live in the camp. It's a company facility for foreigners. It's a little way outside the city, but there aren't so many bombs there. Here, this is your housing card. Room and board will be deducted from your salary." We pick up our passes. And the last word on the lower stamp is indeed "Police."

No, this is not yet the moment where we can simply take a deep breath and relax. It is the time when we must switch to the tried and true, closing offensive. "Just look at us, the way they sent us here. We've lost everything. We haven't got one single piece of decent clothing. We would like to keep our transport instructions. We're going to demand compensation." A civilian official, sitting behind another desk, hands us another ration card. The stamp at the bottom reads *Deutsche Arbeitsfront*, German Workers Front—another charming phrase.

The storehouse of the *Arbeitsfront* is in the factory basement. We hand our ration cards to an elderly man. He hobbles off to the back and then returns with two bundles,which he sets down on the table in front of us. We open one, and Karl counts quietly: "Ten pieces— and look how they're folded and packed—these knots—and these short quilted jackets. Did you sort these, or did I?"

We are then escorted to our work site. We have been assigned to the forge. Everything around us is black, penetrated in places by a yellowish white glow and a cold dark red, the only colors in this huge shop. Like small devils, workers give ground to the tongues of fire lapping at them from the furnaces. With tongs of the most marvelous shapes they thrust and parry and then jump aside, making way for glowing, buttery soft sheets, cubes and cylinders, which will be pressed into a variety of forms, all according to the bite these huge monsters, the drop hammers, will take with every blow. No, we're not working with an all-powerful death here. But still—some of its tools are being kneaded out of this glowing mass. Those pieces over there, the ones that are fading from glowing yellow to dark red and are finally extinguished in blackish gray. They look like housings for large shells, grenades, or something of that sort.

It won't be long before the morning shift is over. For the time being we are only observing, each of us at a different drop hammer. As we are leaving the forge, we meet up with a work crew marching three abreast across the courtyard, accompanied by a guard. These poor men are even more ragtag than we are. There are still some metal uniform buttons hanging from a few of the soiled, tight-fitting green jackets. As they pass by, we can see two large letters, *KG*, on their backs. What was that? You're escaping from *Gefangenschaft*—prison. That's how the old woman had put it. *G*—*Gefangener*—prisoner, *K*—*Krieg*—war, *KG*—*Kriegsgefangener*—prisoner of war. I wonder how good their documents are.

The dormitory is in a village called Seckenheim. To get there we take an electric train, with clean white cars, on a route along the Neckar River. We get out at a point where the countryside approaches the edge of the city. In places there are small, well-tended fields.

"*Stojala, dumala, cihanoczka moloda*—she was standing there, the young gypsy maid . . ." These aren't the barracks, or the green fences, or the pines of Treblinka. But the same wild, polyphonic voices resound from within the rectangular building we are now entering. It looks very much like a country inn. And upstairs, in what used to be the main hall, these young workers are lying on their bunks on their straw mattresses, wandering or standing around, and singing their songs full of life. In contrast to the Ukrainians at Treblinka, these young men, who had volunteered to leave occupied Ukraine for work in the Reich, are in civilian dress. Their faces are pale from factory work. At the big table they're playing cards and pushing *Hrosche*—groschen—back and forth. Someone speaking Polish wants to roll a cigarette, but first he will have to take his tobacco from a large roll and chop it up himself. There's a roll on the table, and it's here for anyone who wants it. Tobacco is grown in this region, and so are wine grapes.

We hear someone asking in Czech: "You're Czechs?" Cautiously at first, and then after we doff our caps in greeting: "I see you boys have been locked up in some hole . . ." We're not worried. Our hair, which is finally growing back in, is proof enough that we're "the right sort." No one will ask any more questions, as long as we don't start in talking about ourselves.

A slender blond man, who doesn't really seem to fit in at all with his fiery fellow Ukrainians, comes up to us and begins speaking in an intently friendly manner: "You're new here. My name is Leo, and I take care of all of the administrative work. Give me your factory passes and your ration cards for room and board. I'll take them to the local police today so that you'll be officially registered. You'll get them all back this evening." There are three other new arrivals today. Two of them appear to be Poles, and one is Dutch.

Of course, foreigners aren't going to be running off on their own to the local police. It's all taken care of in an orderly way. We all work at the factory, one the same as every other. It's important now that the wheels keep rolling. "All Wheels Must Roll for Victory" was the motto we saw several times today, on the factory wall and on the side of the locomotive. That evening Leo hands out police registration cards to all of the new arrivals, certified and stamped. Back home, even before the Germans occupied our country, we had very similar cards, certifying that we were "officially registered at this address."

"Hey, this is a genuine, official document. Now we really do exist. The police have certified it—Vladimir Frysak—Rudolf Masarek."

"Now, if we ever get stopped, we can just say that we had to turn over the rest of our papers at the factory."

"Yes, and we'll have to pick up some nice little case for these identification papers. You must be able to get something like that around here without a ration card."

After a couple of paydays we also manage to get hold of our first decent suit of clothing—without a ration card. Only one of us goes out at a time, while the other lies wrapped in blankets in his bunk back at the dormitory. And now we both have Sunday best, and we can go to the movies together.

We never see a sign reading "No Jews Allowed," not on the door to the movie theater, nor on the door to the local bar, nor at the entrance to the park. It's not necessary. There aren't any more Jews here. This city is *judenrein*—free of Jews.

The first film we went to see, all dressed up and full of excitement, was in color: *Baron von Münchhausen.* I was transfixed at the sight of Hans Albers, whom I knew from his previous leading roles, flying through the middle of a battlefield atop a cannonball, wearing a red jacket, snow-white pants, and shiny black boots that reached up over his knees. So here I sat, a long way from Treblinka, out in life, watching the fanciful adventures of Baron von Münchhausen.

No one should be misled: the smiths at Lanz are not those idealized figures standing there wrapped in leather aprons and hammering away at an anvil all day. Sepp, the man who trained me, first as a stoker and then as a hammer operator, is a large man who looks a lot like a bear. When he walks, his heavy upper body is always leaning so far forward that it looks as if his legs are trying to catch up with him with every step he takes. He also has the voice and, behind his oval glasses, the sly little eyes of an old bear. Still, he does have something about him of the old village smithy who used to shoe our horses back home: he stinks pleasantly of sweat and tinder. Even if he were younger he wouldn't be drafted. As the result of an accident, he lost the index finger of his right hand and would have some difficulty pulling a trigger, and with his flat feet he would hardly be able to lead a charge.

Hans, with tufts of gray hair sticking out from under his old seaman's cap, is so short that the handle of the three-thousand-kilogram drop hammer reaches up to his shoulders when it is set for a full drop. Recently, when the hammer was being set up, a one-ton weight fell on his feet and crushed all ten toes. Since then I have been operating the hammer for the master smith, Sepp. But Anton is the man who has taught me the most. In that short span of time when our shifts change, and he and Otto relieve Karl and me.

Anton is someone special here, because he really does belong in a forging plant. He really is a smith and was trained back home somewhere in northern Bohemia. And he's the only one of us who really has the right build for all of this heavy work. The only thing he lacks is well-tanned skin. Maybe his entire body is so white because he washes himself so carefully. When this strong, elegant craftsman is fully engaged, his big hands appear to be performing a kind of surgery on whatever white-yellow piece he may be gripping with his tongs. After his shift is over and he's in street clothes, he scrubs his shovellike hands until they're pink and look like the hands of a doctor at work in his clinic. His blond, somewhat reddish hair is parted while it's still damp from the showers, and his cap sits at a slight angle on his head. His black oxfords always shine. Anton—Tonda, in Czech—must have an entire closetful of shoeshine supplies at home, just as he does here in his locker.

Otto—Ota, in Czech—is from Moravia. Since he's the one who relieves Karl at the foot hammer in the back row, he and Karl have come to know each other very well. Anton teases them about the "Christmas cookies" they're forging—actually, links for tank tracks—but the backs of their work smocks are covered with white salty "maps" of dried sweat. Everyone working here in the "hot plant" has "maps." If you calculate that during one shift they make eight to nine hundred of those pieces out of long heavy rods, then during that one shift they lift more kilograms, indeed tons, than we do at the heaviest hand-operated hammer.

Of course, Otto is also a trained smith, but he doesn't look the part at all. Compared with Anton, he looks like a lad from some faraway land. He has dark skin and thick black hair, which keeps falling in his face and which he keeps tucking back up under his cap. Every day, both Anton and Otto come to work from Hockenheim, where they live. According to Anton, when they came here in 1942, it was still possible to earn good money and live comfortably—no bombing raids back then. But Otto suggests, with a simple grin, that a girl played some role in Anton's decision. As for Otto himself, you couldn't tell what interested him more and what interested him less. Maybe he hadn't wanted Anton to leave by himself, or maybe he had wanted to earn some money, or maybe he had also wanted to meet some German women.

"Why don't you two get your own place?" Otto asks us once at the end of our shift. "As Czechs, you have a right to it. Only the Ukrainians and the Poles, or anyone else from one of the lesser races, are required to live in the camp."

And Anton adds: "They're really shitting you in that camp. You don't get any ration cards or food coupons there, and all you have to eat is that garbage they serve up. The few Czechs who are still there are either too dumb or too lazy to take care of themselves. There are eight Czechs here in the forging plant, and except for you two we've all managed to find a place to sublet. We all get food allowances for heavy labor, for working in the hot plant." From his old, worn briefcase, which he has hung up next to the hammer, Otto pulls out a half-eaten sandwich smeared thick with *Schmalz*.

"Yes, he's right," we tell ourselves later. "We are loyal Czechs, and we have a right to live on our own and to get our own food coupons. Good God, we're not going to let ourselves be suckered. We're going to get what we're entitled to. And women aren't off limits for loyal Czechs either . . ."

Before we move out of the camp, we arrange a little farewell party. We get thirty liters of wine from a vintner in the Pfalz, and our handsome Leo manages to conjure up the bread and *Schmalz*. And then we really start to celebrate: "Oj pri luczku, pri luczku." Together with these wild Ukrainians we're singing about a fiery steed galloping free across the broad plains and fields, and about a cossack who was not so free—without letting anyone know how we actually came to know this song. Leo confides to us that he got the bread and the *Schmalz* from an innkeeper's wife here in the neighborhood and that he often visits her when he's got time on his hands.

Moving is like living through the deluge, my grandmother used to say. But our move is an easy one. We simply carry our two little suitcases and our two margarine boxes the few blocks to our new residence. Seckenheim is a small village. The street where we now live is on the edge of Seckenheim and is actually only half a street: there are only houses on one side. From our upstairs window we look directly out on the fields. The tobacco plot in front of our house belongs to our landlord. He has also dug out an air raid shelter here and reinforced it with wooden beams. His bunker reminds me of the World War I trenches I have seen in pictures and always liked so much.

I check myself over to see if I am clean enough to get into a real bed, and I am amazed that the white sheets and the red and white comforter are so pristine. No stains, no bloody smears. I am amazed that everything on the table in our room is exactly where we left it— the whole time we're at the factory. And not a thing in our wardrobe has been touched.

Recently, when Karl had the morning shift and I didn't have to go to work until that afternoon, I lay alone in my bed and didn't move a muscle. But with my eyes I felt the comforter, the blanket, and the walls; with my ears I savored the silence. I stood at the window for a time, in *my* pajamas, and blinked at the snowless, rusty brown winter fields. Yes, this is what is known as *Privat*. We are living in private accommodations.

This little upstairs room belonged to the sons of our landlord, Herr Gottfried K., and his wife. The two boys slept in these two beds until they were old enough for uniforms. One of the sons will never sleep here again, and the other won't sleep here again until the war is over, if then. So the old folks decided to rent out the upstairs room. In contrast to all the others who can't find a way to spend their worthless wartime money, these two retirees don't even have enough of that. But when the Winter Aid Society came calling with a money box and bag to collect donations for the soldiers at the front, old Herr K. didn't even bother to refer to his financial condition: "I've already made a donation. My donation fell somewhere near Kremenchug" is all he said.

We often hear things like this from our landlord. It's hard to say whether this is the way he's always felt, or whether it's because he just doesn't care anymore, now that he's lost a son and had to leave his work as a master mason because of his ulcer. At the same time our landlord is failing, his wife has become wrinkled with worry. She takes care of everything and everyone, because there is a certain way things must be done, and if anything were to be neglected then things would just get much worse.

"Young people like you should eat at least one good meal a day, especially when you have to work so hard. You can fix whatever you'd like here in the kitchen. I'll show you which pots and pans to use, and I'll check to see that the stove doesn't get too hot. And you make sure you take the time to eat off plates and use the silverware in the drawer over there, and sit down here at the table where it's warm and you can eat your meal in peace. Of course you'll wash the dishes when you're done, and put everything back in its place. And if you're here when there's an air raid alert, then you get your things and come into the bunker with us."

Yes, yes—and you won't be making any mess upstairs when you're down here in the kitchen where I have to sweep the floor every day anyway. And we won't be having to heat that room if all you do up there is sleep. Our boys didn't fool around up there any more than necessary either. Now, when there's an air raid alert, you two can help us with our things too, and if anything gets hit, then we'll all have to help put the fires out and save what we can save. In any event, you won't be staying in the house if there's a siren blowing. I can just imagine the kind of problems I'd be having with the officials if something were to happen to either of you while you're staying in this house . . . Maybe these are the thoughts that are really racing around in my landlady's mind, under that little bun. But maybe that's not at all what she's thinking and I'm just an asshole for putting those thoughts in her head. If her hair were already gray, and what's even more absurd, if the skin underneath had turned into dry little scales, then she'd be ready, just like that other one and . . . Well, Frau K., why don't you just take my arm, and I'll walk with you—to the doctor, to the infirmary . . .

Today an alert brings us all together again just as one shift is relieving another. Down in the shower room I am sitting next to Karl, who is already in his work clothes, and watching Anton and Otto showering at the end of their shift. Heinrich Toman has joined us. He's the oldest and most experienced of all the Czechs in the forging plant, and maybe in the whole complex. His hair is gray but still very thick, and he combs it straight back. He is as slender as a rod. If, instead of his once blue but now oily black overalls, he were wearing a pair of gray slacks, oxfords, a sports jacket, an open shirt, and a scarf, if he had washed the splotches of soot from his face, shaved, and maybe even dusted his face lightly with powder, setting off his white hair and bright blue eyes, then Heinrich would be an elegant older gentleman who had spent many years in exotic lands and was now living out his days with his many memories. Heinrich enjoys the reputation of being the best crane operator in the plant. At those times when there are heavy weights to install, or whenever the help of a crane is needed, every hammer operator is reassured when he can look up and see Heinrich's beret-topped head in the crane cabin.

"You two," Heinrich turns to us, "they put you two through the wringer and then, in passing, suggested that you might like to volunteer for work in the Reich. From the way you looked when you got here . . . Don't worry, we're not trying to drag anything out of you. We're all volunteers here. I had to get away from my last guest engagement, fast and far. And Otto—admit it, you scoundrel, back home you couldn't get rid of your virginity fast enough, and then you made tracks for the German Reich."

"You've got my confession, Mr. Toman." Otto is the only one who doesn't address Heinrich by his first name. "But why don't you tell us what you've got going with Thomas Pech. They say that you've made an agreement with the foreman, that after a twelve-hour shift you'll always relieve each other, because you share a set of false teeth and you hand them off at the time clock."

"I help out Thomas Pech because it was a flying pig from the Pilsen slaughterhouse that got the poor man sent here. One day, for some reason, one of the German occupation troops was walking along the outside wall of the municipal slaughterhouse in Pilsen. And there, all of a sudden, in the fading evening light, half a pig carcass comes flying over the wall and lands at his feet. No ration card, no food coupons were attached. And that is when Thomas, then employed at the Pilsen slaughterhouse, decided to volunteer for work in the German Reich, already known as the Third. And while they were preparing him for his new job, he seems to have misplaced some of his teeth."

Anton turns off the water and carefully works himself over with his towel. He aims his questions at the two of us: "What do you do about women, when you've got your landlord and landlady at home? I can't imagine that they allow you to take anyone up to your room. I guess you have to go out."

"They haven't got an arrangement like yours—the landlady at home alone, and the landlord out on some unknown battlefield. But you can be sure that, in its own good time, something interesting will come your way. Germany has been depopulated of its men, and the bombs keep falling thicker and faster." Heinrich sets a tobacco tin down on the bench beside him, opens it, tears apart and crushes two cigarette butts, and then mixes the old tobacco with the contents of the tin. He doesn't start talking again until he's rolling a new cigarette between his fingers: "And you know, they're all curious about every piece of meat they haven't yet seen. A piece of meat that weighs less than a pound, it's even less than that Venetian merchant demanded.

"How old are you, Otto—twenty? I'm forty-eight. That's something like two times twenty-four, but in some ways it isn't. You think first before you shoot your gun, even if it's loaded. I don't know any housewife who can make me a goulash as good as my own, and mine's getting old now, anyway."

"Mine's not so young anymore, either, but she's very pretty," Anton says. "She takes care of everything. I give her all the food coupons and the ration cards. She always makes my lunch when I go to work, and when I get back home there's always a warm meal."

"My old lady always gets wine for Saturday night," Otto chimes in. "Look, I've got her old man's socks."

"Well, well, just look at you," Heinrich observes. "The other one's fighting for you at the front, and when he gets back he won't find a pair of his own socks in his dresser. Actually, if you look at it that way, this is your historic mission in this war. Your lady, your old woman, will tell her grandchildren, if she has any, that Czechs are really very pleasant fellows. If it were up to me, we'd have more foreigners in this country, and they should be spending more of their nights lying in the arms of lonesome women, whispering back and forth—hold me tight, love me, until the bombs or the end of the war do us part."

The all clear is sounded, Otto and Anton go home, and I stoke up the furnace again. During the alert it had been set to the lowest possible temperature and had cooled down from glowing yellow to a dark red.

Karl gets ready to look in on Herta, who works in the shop, and he picks up something for lunch and for his afternoon break. In the meantime I carry our suitcases and margarine boxes downstairs and into the hallway. Our landlord and landlady have also set out their most valuable possessions. Whenever there is an alert, all of these things are carried out into the little bunker. When we are at home, we can get it all done in a flash. But when we're at work, our landlord has to carry everything himself. It is then that we think of him as our Diamond Bearer, without his being in the least aware of his esteemed role. He doesn't know anything about the contents of the shaving kit in my suitcase.

I look out the window to see if Karl is on his way back. Today he seems to be in a hurry, and he doesn't even bother to show me how full Herta has packed the little paper sack. He's waving a newspaper around in the air. He comes storming through the door and shoves the front page into my face: "They've Landed" is the headline. When? Yesterday. The newspaper is dated 7 June 1944.

Landed—already here—on this side—on these shores. You Allied boys, get here as fast as you can, and be careful that you don't step on any of those mines I've been forging . . .

❀

Those Strange Chamber Pots on Their Heads

During one of the bombing raids in January 1945, the roof was blown off the forge. Since then we have been working as roofers. Our foreman sent us up the ladders to train with the "real" roofers. They are French prisoners of war, who, with the passing of time, have nothing left of their bluish gray uniforms but their heavy overcoats and—only a very few of them—the berets on their heads. It may be that they aren't all real roofers. But they volunteered for this work because there wouldn't be any supervisors looking over their shoulders up at these heights. When the next bombing raid blew off our new roof, the Françoises, Pierres, and Claudes, the guys with the home-rolled glow sticks hanging from the corners of their mouths, didn't show up. Maybe, at what was once the main hall of the inn but is now a dormitory, somewhere in Schriesheim, Oggersheim, or Viernheim, they took a direct hit.

Now we are up here by ourselves. There aren't any master roofers chasing around after us. We—again that's Anton, Otto, Heinrich, Karl, and me. Up on the roof, twelve meters above a floor of cast-iron plates, we feel like athletes or actors. We walk across beams and newly constructed framing spanning the entire width of the plant, and toss roof tiles to each other, competing to see whose bright red tile will trace the most elegant arc through the air.

After about an hour of such amusement, we crawl out behind the skylight, onto a flat space where it is difficult to see us from below, and we warm ourselves in the sun. Right now, in the middle of February, it is as lovely here on the Rhine as it is at home in the spring.

No one notices us as we observe what's going on below. The entire forge has been shut down. The furnace openings are black; the drop hammers are silent. No fire, no blow upon blow, no bright crackling coke embers anywhere, not even the dark red glow of

forged pieces beginning to cool. Nothing but cold, gray iron everywhere, expectant calm—the little people below are standing around
behind the tall hammers and furnaces where they cannot easily be
seen, debating, loafing, insignificant and expendable.

Two female figures enliven the scene: "Look at that hothouse
flower, Luise—how old is she? Eighteen, nineteen? She was out looking for it. You know: 'I don't want to be a virgin when the bomb hits.'"

"But Gerda, now there's a real tough broad, well endowed fore
and aft. In her twenty-five years she's already had more than her
share of well-fought battles."

"You say she's a tough broad. Well then, how did she get herself
into this nice little mess? No one noticed at first, until word got out
that she was especially fond of the Pole who operates the foot hammer in the second block. A German woman and a Polish man—that
is clearly a punishable offense. Just a little while ago Annemarie
brought a copy of the official regulations and read them out loud to
us. To sleep with a Pole is a serious breach of the racial purity law,
and that goes for Ukrainians too, and if you're caught with a Russian—they're all prisoners of war—you'd probably be stoned on the
spot. But back to Gerda: she was seen through the office window
crying, ample breasts rising and falling with each sob. It was the
assistant director, the political one, who really started to scream. He's
the one who's always wearing that little cookie on his lapel and chasing after women. The incident was covered up. And it seems that
Gerda had a pretty good idea of how to do penance."

I stop listening. A few old memories resurface. I now know how
to operate all of the drop hammers down there. I have worked at all
of the large furnaces, and I know how to adjust them and get the
iron hot without using too much coke. I wanted to understand
everything, and it made me feel like a whole person. I liked learning
this work. I like being here. When I was back home I used to think
that Germany was one big wasteland, that very little grew here, that
everyone was gloomy and all the women were ugly. And from back
there, from my life in the camp, until I escaped with Karl, I could
not imagine a German without a skull and crossbones. But maybe it
is only because of that inferno that everything here looks so good—
even the glow at the furnaces and the hammers that takes your
breath away. Maybe that's why this piece of Germany seems like one

big garden to me—with a few factories scattered around here and there. Or maybe it truly is good fortune that brought us to the Rhine. "Rhine—Women—Wine." It rhymes.

High overhead, so high that you can hardly see them in the light of the sun, there are fighters flying by at regular intervals. And then we hear the prolonged roar of heavier planes. We cannot depend on the sirens anymore. The Americans, the English, and the French are supposed to have already reached the banks of the Rhine in places. Their planes get here before the sirens sound.

Suddenly there is a penetrating whine overhead, and it's getting more and more piercing. Something is rushing in at us, pushing us down flat on the roof. We are lying face down, our heads between our arms. The whine is interrupted by sharp, percussive bursts. They have never been here before, but now they are here—the low-level bombers. We raise our heads as the roar slowly fades away. We have to see what's happened to the plant.

Heinrich is standing in front of the statue of the founder in the company courtyard. He's in his oil- and soot-smeared overalls with his beret on his head, and his pose echoes the stance of old Heinrich Lanz: one foot forward, his right hand inside his coat. "Look, it was a clean shot, and he's still standing. I don't think I'd ever be able to do that. Well, this is the end game, boys. Have you ever played chess? Do you know the vocabulary of chess? Not very likely, since you did not often make your way directly from the theater to the café. So I'll explain what comes next, and that's what we in chess call a technical checkmate."

Each day fewer and fewer workers show up at the forge. Even the Russian prisoners with the letters *KG* on their backs are absent. There are no more Italian hats worn by the bersaglieri. Their feathers had already been clipped by the time they arrived here at the end of 1944, when they no longer wanted to fight in alliance with the Germans.

Streetcars are no longer running, nor are the trains. There hasn't been a sign of either Anton or Otto for days. We walk from Seckenheim to the factory for the sole purpose of looking around and checking up on old Heinrich. It used to take us twenty minutes to get to Mannheim on the OEG line, but now it takes three hours to make our way through all the air raids and the chaos in the streets. The city has been depopulated. Everyone has left; they're all in hiding. And I sense that they're waiting, we're waiting, for something. For what? For the men beyond the Rhine. For them to get here, for everything to be over. My God, what will that be like—the end and, for us, a beginning? Nonsense. I can't let myself start imagining or even thinking about it.

We come upon Heinrich in front of his house near the factory, and he's clearing a path to the front door and into his apartment on the ground floor of what used to be a two-story building. He has pushed aside only the largest pieces of rubble and debris, working his way through piles of brick, plaster, and splintered glass. He is the only person to be seen in this desolate, wasted street. We decide that he should move in with us in the less dangerous area outside the city. We ourselves had recently moved a short distance to new quarters in Seckenheim. Dear old Frau K. really had mothered us too much and left us too little free space. Our new landlady had moved her children into the countryside a few days before and turned over an entire three-room apartment to us. So we have plenty of room.

We immediately start packing Heinrich's possessions. "Heinrich, at our place in Seckenheim the panes of glass are still in one piece, and you can look through them out onto the fields. Where did you ever get so many suitcases and so many things?"

"Well, when the women here found out that their men weren't coming back, or sometimes if they simply hadn't heard anything for a long time, then they came and brought these things. One would bring one thing, another something else. When I comforted them they could see that there was a good and gentle soul hiding behind this worn exterior." Heinrich ties his suitcases onto a two-wheeled cart. "Apparently I earned this vehicle when the last of the ladies moved out."

"Annemarie's going to move in with us, too, early tomorrow. She has a bicycle, and it's still in good shape, but she doesn't have anything to eat. And there isn't a single crumb anywhere in our spacious quarters."

While searching for food in a bombed-out section of the city, we find our way into the basement of a sizable house and are immediately transported by a wonderful fragrance. "My dear friends, they've taken the grub with them, but they couldn't carry the wine, so they tapped the barrels and just let it run out."

"Or maybe someone got here before us?"

"No matter, they say wine is nourishing, even by itself. You don't have guzzle it right out of the barrels. There are still a few unopened bottles."

As we leave the cellar and come back out into the sunlight, blinking, we suddenly hear a whine overhead, accompanied by the staccato rat-a-tat-tat of a machine gun. "Now you see what your wine bottles are good for—just look how fast you fall to the ground."

Karl is lying on his stomach with his wine bottles under his arms. In the next cellar we come to, he lets them drop and smash on the floor. There are two large bottles in wicker baskets. "Damn it, how many cellars have we been in today? Five, six? And everywhere we go, all we find is wine. Nothing but wine and more wine. And not a single crumb of dry bread to dunk in it."

On the broken-down walls that no longer divide anything, protect anything, belong to anything, walls that are no longer walls, signs and slogans blur into one another before my eyes: "Every Wheel Must Turn for Victory," "The Enemy Is Listening," "Father Dead. Werner with Family in the Black Forest," "Celui qui pille, sera comdamné à mort," "Looters Will Be Sentenced to Death," "Ein Volk, ein Reich, ein Führer."

You beast, here I stand looking down on you from these heaps of rubble, getting drunk on your wine, and at the sight of your getting smashed to hell. Do you know who I am, who we are? Do you know what evidence we carry with us and in us? And now, now it has been given to us to witness your end and your agony.

Stop, wait. It cannot be possible that I am seeing what I see. So there was once a lovely single-family house on this site. On the first floor there was a kitchen, a dining room, and a living room. On the second floor there were bedrooms and a bath. But I can't see the house anymore; all I can see is a drainage pipe attached to a bathtub on the second floor—nothing but a bathtub—and there is another smaller pipe leading away from the tub down into the ground. No one can live here anymore, but they could bathe, if they could somehow climb up to the tub. All right, let's move, move, loosen up, faster, faster—to the bath, to the disinfecting bath, here's hoping that the water's not too cold.

Of course we might have known that no one would trade food

for wine. All we've been able to get is a few cigarettes. We sit at home in the dark. We heat the place with our little iron stove, because now, at the end of March, the evenings are still cool and the cigarettes have to be dried, and we should be having something warm for dinner—mulled wine, what else. Outside it's beginning to thunder and whine; the sky is being torn into glowing shreds, framed in red, blue, and shimmering yellow. "That's artillery fire. They've already moved in with their artillery."

There are now three of us, no longer just two. The odds for one in three are better than the odds for one in two. And there could be no more appropriate backdrop for the story we're going to tell Heinrich now. "Heinrich, take a good, big drink and listen. Hear our testimony—make it yours—in case the two of us . . ."

By the time the stillness outside—we don't know when it set in—is broken by the first birdsong announcing the dawn, Heinrich knows everything. He knows about the terminus enclosed in green fencing, about the train station with the sign that reads "Treblinka," about the disinfecting bath with its deadly gas, about the "infirmary" with the Red Cross insignia. He knows the names of everyone in the SS special commando at Treblinka, the real names as well as the nicknames. He knows about the uprising on 2 August 1943. Heinrich is standing next to the little iron stove. Now and then he adds a piece of a chopped-up chair to the fire, causing the dimly lit room to be suffused with a red light. Occasionally he runs his fingers over the cigarettes lined up on a stool. He chooses the driest one and lights up.

"So you guys are Jews. Who would have believed that—in the forge, stoking the furnaces and operating the hammers. And you say that there were probably a million—and you might be the only two . . . ?"

A strange noise tears us out of the slumber we're enjoying in the warmth of the stove. There are all kinds of people rushing past our windows, with carts, rucksacks, and baskets. And working her way through the middle of this current, headed in our direction, we can see Annemarie pushing her bicycle. She has two suitcases, one tied to the carrier and the other tied to the handlebars. "Everyone's going to the switching yard. There are supposed to be entire bombed-out trains there, train cars full of food," she explains as we're carrying her suitcases and her bicycle into the apartment. Woe unto us, if we ever leave a bicycle out of our sight! Even if we locked it up in the back yard, it could disappear in a flash.

"So, good friends, let's go, with the help of our two-wheeled fighter bomber . . ."

"In the meantime Annemarie can keep the fire going."

The switching yard is one of the smaller freight stations on the edge of the city, and from here the best way to get there is a shortcut through the fields. The American boys have had some success with this target. If they had missed by as little as a kilometer in our direction, then right now we probably wouldn't have any apartment or any appetite at all. As we're crossing the pedestrian bridge headed for an intermediary stairway that leads down to the tracks, a grand scene is unfolding: boxes and crates covered with soot and dust are pouring out of wrecked and rocking cars. No one knows whom they are from and whom they are for, these huge quantities of no-man's possessions, threatened by confusion and rot.

It is no longer possible to tell which doors blew off in an explosion and which were broken open by human hands. Heinrich is standing on the running board in front of one of the smashed sliding doors. The car is full of hats. Heinrich picks up one after the other and yells to Karl and me in turn: "How about this one—or this—or that?" The hats sail majestically through the air, and Heinrich, the actor from the Bohemian provinces in the pose of a grand seigneur, begins to recite the ballad of Cyrano de Bergerac: "I throw my broad hat hither, and that with grace."

Two cars on the opposite track rise up and collapse onto each other like two thrashing stallions. A woman, her face and her hair powdered with flour, looking like a lady of the Rococo, is holding two small white sacks to her bosom. She speaks to a young boy and seems to be promising him both. The next car is lying on its back like a dead cow on a chain.

Wait, what have we here in this car? English labels on boxes of yellow powder: dried eggs. Cartons of cigarettes, Lucky Strike. In the other half of this compartment there are two cases of bottles in wicker baskets—treason—wine, more wine, but we don't have any of this kind yet: Chianti! They probably confiscated this in Italy. And now we'll confiscate it. Or is it—was it a Red Cross shipment? Doesn't matter. We could use some Red Cross assistance, couldn't we?

Green uniforms appear up on the embankment; shots ring out. The train yard empties quickly. Someone says that the two foreigners who are lying on the embankment near the pedestrian bridge were hit by low-flying fighters. Someone else claims that they were shot by the militia, which had just rushed to the scene. "Looters will be . . ."

This little yellow mound—how many eggs could this be, twenty, thirty? Let's see, let's mix it together with the margarine Annemarie has managed to get hold of in the meantime. Twenty, thirty scrambled eggs, Chianti Mellini in a lovely wicker basket, and all of this without one piece of bread or one single potato. We all slide around on our chairs. Karl is swinging an empty bottle by its woven handle. Heinrich is almost as teary-eyed as he was when he was bombed out in that air raid.

"They were carrying off flour and potatoes right under our noses, while I was fooling around with those damn hats. And we shouldn't have left just because the green guys arrived. Jesus Christ, there must be eggs and flour somewhere in those cars. Annemarie should not want for things like that."

"Heinrich, it's going to be dark in no time. We're not going to make it back tonight. They'll pick us off just like they did those two this afternoon."

"You're not afraid, are you?"

"Who, me?"

"But one of us should stay here with Annemarie and watch the apartment. Two can take care of this expedition."

Karl stays; Heinrich and I go. It is soon evening. In front of us the road through the fields is quiet and deserted, as is the entire area. About halfway along we see uniformed figures hunched down in the bushes. "This must be the grandpas and the little boys in the *Volkssturm*, the civil militia, and probably a few regulars who got here this morning. Didn't look particularly dangerous, actually looked pretty fagged out. But we can't turn around now."

"Halt, what are you doing here?"

"We'll be straight with you. We work at the Lanz plant and live near here. Back home we haven't got a bite to eat, and we thought maybe we could find something in those bombed-out cars at the switching yard. This morning we saw people bringing things back from there . . ."

"That was this morning, but now this evening there's been American fire coming in on the pedestrian bridge."

"But . . ." With a wave of his hand, Heinrich interrupts and follows the old man's glance, which is turned toward our vehicle. In order to make it more maneuverable we've attached only one shaft instead of the usual two. "Good, huh?"

"Yeah, pretty clever." The two-wheeler has made fellow countrymen of us. "Okay, go—who gives a shit anyway!"

The closer we get to the pedestrian bridge, the louder our cart seems to squeak. We pick it up and carry it quietly down the stairs. As we slip from car to car it seems to me for a moment that someone has just come rushing across the bridge. I signal Heinrich. We hide in one of the cars just behind the sliding door and wait.

"In this stillness it is easy to imagine that there are some characters out there lugging their heads around under their arms." Heinrich grows silent, and then begins to grumble: "Oh no, no, no, this just can't be, but it is, man, now I really do believe that the powers of darkness are playing games with us—this bottle, this huge bottle, packed in wood shavings, is full of spiritus—pure spirit alcohol—about twenty-five liters or so, but not a single spud, not one single potato. We'll get something good to eat in exchange for this spiritus—but not tonight."

Once we're back up on the bridge, we lift the bottle into the cart. Using the shaft, I push and steer from the back, and Heinrich steadies the bottle, holding it by the neck. "What are we going to say to our friends in uniform when they ask what we've got here instead of potatoes?"

"That we've taken it for them, and for us, to use as a disinfectant. It's possible they're not even there anymore, that they've gone home—to mama, for a good night's sleep."

Along the way, between the bridge and the few isolated houses, our cart creates such a racket in the thick, heavy stillness that we almost have to converse out loud. "Halt"—even though it's restrained and not very loud, it stops us in our tracks. "Hands . . ." this quiet but express command cannot mean anything other than Hands up!

We turn toward the voice. From an opening where there must have once been a window on the ground floor, a few small rings flash our way. Okay, hands up—if I drop the shaft, the cart will lose its equilibrium, and the bottle will slide off—crash, boom—and they'll shoot. So I raise my left hand, my free hand, first, and then I slowly raise my right hand, so that I can grab the shaft again if I have to. All the while I am tracking Heinrich's hands. One is already over his head, and he's raising the other, the one holding the neck of the bottle, so adroitly that he's able first to slide the bottle slowly down off the cart. That's good. Now I can finally set the shaft down, and we have all of our hands above our heads.

"Hey." It sounds and looks as if we're supposed to move closer. One, two, three steps, in the dim light of the little house the figures begin to assume a more distinct shape.

"What are they wearing on their heads . . ." Standing next to me, Heinrich begins to stutter, "What kind of strange chamber pots? It's really them, isn't it!"

My God—how do you say *shoot* in English—"Don't shoot. Czechs." Did I get it right, or not? It doesn't matter. They're not going to shoot. One of them is signaling us to follow him behind the house, and they point their stubby weapons at us again when we try to embrace them. We can't make ourselves understood in English. I only know a few words. But one of them is speaking some tortured version of what sounds like Polish: "*Kde*—where—*Nemcy*—Germans?"

The darkness over our heads is pierced by an iridescent projectile, and then a second comes flying in, and a third, then an entire swarm. Streaks of light fill the sky and form bright glowing arcs overhead. We run through the gardens behind the single-family houses. We know that the individual plots are separated by low-strung wires rather than fences. But our Americans don't know it. The slight young man with the woven straps attached to his holster, the one who's being led by Heinrich, keeps tripping over these wires. As the Germans return fire, Heinrich pulls the soldier up and yells enthusiastically into his face in Czech: "Well—are you that drunk, or am I?" Most of the Germans in uniform really have gone home—to mama, to sleep. A few of the ones who had stayed behind, including several civilians from nearby houses, have been herded into a cellar room by the Americans. We are taken into another room where we think we may find some food. All we get from them is cigarettes. And we'll spend the night in the cellar.

"*Prosze*—please," says the one who knows a little Polish, as he offers us a light. Now, for the first time, I can see that the face under that large helmet—which looks very different from German helmets—is very young. He must be younger than I am. He picked up a few words of Polish from his father when he, still a young lad, went with his parents to America. Shall I now open my arms to this boy with that strange chamber pot on his head, and reveal to him what has happened in the country that is also his father's country? Insanity, nonsense—the only thing he cares about now is not getting killed himself. We hear a roar overhead. The door closes behind us, and Heinrich and I are alone in the cellar.

"Rudolf, tell me that after all those liters of wine, you're hungry for nothing but fruit preserves—cherries, plums, pears." With the help of a lit match Heinrich is inspecting shelves full of canning jars, both empty and full. "Now this is a housekeeper, man. What a wife she'd make! Well, maybe not, on second thought. She'd be keeping a very close eye on everything; she'd have me on a very short leash. These are last year's preserves. She counted everything and rationed it out over the entire year. And now we'll collect, two shelves full, and we'll take down the boards so we don't have to sleep on this bare cement floor. But we'll have to be on our feet first thing tomorrow morning, because if what I'm thinking is right, this forward unit won't be here for very long."

When Heinrich wakes me at dawn, everything is quiet. The Americans are nowhere to be seen. We open the door to the room where the Germans are assembled. They are sitting quietly on benches, their backs to one another. They don't know that the door is open again. The Americans must have unlocked it before they left.

"What's going to happen to us?" the old woman asks. Apparently she's also speaking for the old man seated next to her. Most of them had seen us with the Americans last evening.

So what's going to happen to them is just what we say is going to happen: "Nothing, nothing is going to happen to you, as long as you sit there quietly until we say . . ." Nothing is going to happen to you, but a little disinfectant will be sprayed into this chamber through the air vents in the ceiling. That's the thought that comes to mind.

Heinrich shuts the door and turns the key again. "And now we've got about an hour to look around for some potatoes." We run up the

steps into the living quarters on the floor above. Comforters and
mattresses slit open, stained with blood, cupboards torn open, the
door to the pantry—it had probably been locked—broken open,
everything run through with a bayonet, destruction everywhere,
everything trampled, dirty, sticky, and covered with little white
feathers.

"This is the way a soldier secures his position when his back isn't
covered, so there won't be any surprises from any direction." One of
them must have been wounded. We could hear him all the way
down in the cellar room. "And maybe they went into a rage because
someone from the home guard fired on them." Heinrich picks up a
pair of binoculars that has been left on one of the beds. He looks it
over, reads the label: "Paris. He must have lifted this in France, or
got it on the black market, not knowing that it would end up with a
pack of Bohemians. And look at this, the only things they took out
of the pantry were the eggs. These are eggshells. Everything else might
have been poisoned—for them, but not for us. Look how they
spoiled this *Schmalz* and trampled the flour bags, the pigs." As we
gather the discarded, half-smoked cigarettes, Heinrich's anger at the
Americans abates: "Hey, I'd take a job sweeping up after this army."

By the light of dawn Heinrich is pushing the two-wheeled cart
laden with potatoes, flour, and peas, everything in little sacks and
bags. The jars full of preserves, along with anything else that is
breakable, are being transported in the baby carriage we found in the
cellar. So this road through the fields is the celebrated road to free-
dom, and from behind my baby carriage I am leading the victory
march.

Karl and Annemarie race out of the house to meet us. Looking
out over the fields and the collapsed houses, you can see heavy
American tanks rolling along the main highway. From a second floor
window, in the building that had until now housed French prisoners
of war, a French tricolor is hanging out in front of a cluster of people. The flag is so large that it almost envelops the passing soldiers
who are looking up from their tank hatches.

"Vladimir, I mean: Karl!"

"Rudolf, no: Richard!"

"Yes, yes, Annemarie, only I am still your Heinrich—always your
Heinrich."

A Villa in One of the Finer Quarters

Karl and I are questioned for two days. We give our testimony in a villa in Neuostheim, the elegant suburb we had always known as an intermediate stop on the stretch of tracks between Seckenheim and Mannheim. Heinrich might have worn uniforms like these onstage, these uniforms who are asking us questions and listening to our story. They are so clean, the pants impeccably creased, and the golden letters *US* and *CIC* glisten from their collars. During meal breaks they take us with them to their canteen. My God, how can anyone surrounded by so much food eat so little?

The whole bunch of them are unhealthy, not normal people. "That comes from all of this intelligence business and all of those papers," Heinrich says, when we tell him what went on. "What do they call it? CIC—Counter Intelligence Corps? So they are intelligence types—you can tell by the way they wear their uniforms." In some ways they really are rather odd. Who in the world has ever seen anyone smoke just the tip of the cigarette, a section about as large as a butt, and then throw away the part that would normally be smoked?

After our statements have been taken, we are escorted to another, more elegant room. There we find two higher-ranking officers. One of them is holding a typewritten page in his hand, and they're both reading it. In the meantime the other one is tossing a few words in our direction. What did I hear? That sounded like Yiddish. This high-ranking officer speaks like the Jews spoke in Poland, in Treblinka. "And you didn't learn to pray? You didn't learn Hebrew either?" The officer is looking straight at us. Well, hello—he's not so sure he believes us. And the other one's going to test our Hebrew. Oh, my blessed grandfather, you who counted up all of my sins that Rosh Hashanah when I came running into the temple with Pepi Horak, the goy, neither of us wearing a yarmulke, both of us chewing on horsemeat sausage, Grandfather, you who lay before me in your own excrement in the ghetto of Theresienstadt, your veins slit open, help me to remember now. How was that, how did that go when we gave Him thanks on Friday evening, on the Sabbath? I know I learned that, because I was pleased that we not only thanked Him for bread but also for wine.

"*Boruch ato adonaj . . . hamauzi lechem min haorec*—that's for the bread. *Baure peri hagofen*—that's for the wine." I never was able to write it correctly, don't even know how the syllables go. Maybe the officer-Kapo here didn't understand a word of it, maybe he's used to a different pronunciation? Now he's turning to the other one, who appears to be an even bigger Kapo, and says it's "okay."

"So on this day, you have finally won. You have given your testimony. Just wait and see, you're going to be famous, and from now on I'm going to have to stick with you," Heinrich says, working through his thoughts after dinner.

Later that evening there seems to be some kind of celebration going on in the street and in our stairway downstairs. Two of the boys, probably on patrol, find their way up to our apartment. We don't seem to be able to communicate very well. We try to explain that we're Czechs, not Germans. It seems that both of them are from New York. We pat each other on the back, and they start patting Annemarie too. Then, as if on command, they turn their automatic pistols on us. They don't put their helmets, those silly chamber pots, back on their heads. Instead they beat us with them. One of them shoves his pistol into Annemarie's chest, so hard that she screams and doubles over. Then he grabs her by the hair and drags her off to the stairway. The other one turns out the lights and trains the beam of his flashlight on us. We hear moaning and sobbing coming from the hall. I can hardly tell when one stops and the other begins. Then the beam of light disappears, followed by the sound of boots stomping away. Annemarie drags herself back up the stairs through the darkness and the silence.

They had forced her onto a window seat in the stairway and raped her, one after the other. It happened last night. And now it is early morning. Annemarie is sitting on a stool in the middle of an empty room. She is holding a dishpan in her lap and sorting dried peas. We have never spent this much time in this room before. We had only been using it as a storeroom for the food and wine we managed to appropriate. It pains us to see Annemarie sitting there leaning over a bowl. So we sit down and start sorting too.

My God, can't she lift her head up for just a moment? She needs to move, she needs to stop picking through those peas in the bowl. Damn it . . . Now she's standing up and carrying the sorted peas off, with an expression on her face that is so serene, it's as if she sacrificed herself for us. And maybe we should be thankful to her so that she can have the upper hand. Damn it. And this is supposed to be a victory?

"Well, what did happen? Nothing," Karl starts in. "Did anyone cut off her tits, the way they did back there—in the ghettos? Did they slaughter her mother, father, and brother, one after the other—as they did mine? Why should I worry about her? Why should I worry about any of them?"

"Okay, okay, let off a little steam." Heinrich is picking through a small mound of tobacco and cigarette butts that he has spread out on a piece of old newspaper in front of him. "It doesn't matter at all that she's a German, and we're Czechs, and they're Americans. This is war, they're soldiers, she's a woman, and we're lousy rotten civilians. As far as I know, from my experience, they might just as well have shot us because of her, and not because we were strolling around in front of the German lines. The two of them knew what they were going to do, and maybe their superior officer knew it too and was just hanging around somewhere downstairs. Things like this usually happen at night, when one patrol relieves another. I'll bet those two are a long way away from here tonight. And no one has got a thing on them. In cases like this, not even those gentlemen officers in elegant villas can help."

Heinrich is silent for a while. "That'd be some piece of theater: two men escape from Treblinka, two out of a million, and die at the hands of their liberators, trying to defend the honor of a woman from the enemy camp. Insane, absurd—it's all simply, utterly absurd. I'm furious that I didn't sense something rotten right away, when those two first came in." Heinrich picks at the cigarette he has just rolled. "What's keeping us here anyway? Why don't we move into one of the more elegant quarters? The gentlemen told you to keep yourselves available and not to leave the vicinity. So now you will tell them, that for security reasons, you intend to move even closer. There are plenty of bombed-out villas in the neighborhood. We'll simply take one over."

We load all of our belongings into the two-wheeled cart, onto Annemarie's bicycle, and into the baby carriage we found on that historic night. The wheels on the baby carriage soon give way under the weight of the load; we pull it and push it down the street as if it were a sled. Heinrich stumbles and struggles with the cart shaft to keep his cargo balanced. Annemarie is pushing the weighed-down bicycle and laughing.

The CIC officers didn't say much when we told them we wanted to move into their neighborhood. It would be "all right," they said, adding that they would send someone to take care of us.

The next day a jeep pulls up in front of our one-story "Villa" with its sagging roof and bullet-pocked walls. A scrawny, not very young and not very old man gets out. He might very well have been folded over several times inside this ample uniform. The helmet—the pot —makes an especially amusing impression in his case, because his head is so small. "I am a rabbi in this army," he begins saying in broken German-Yiddish, "who, besides praying, looks out for the welfare of Jewish soldiers, and if you don't mind, I will also be your rabbi."

We are still standing in front of the house, looking at the white letters spelling out *chaplain* on the side of the jeep. "Headquarters decided," he explains, "that there should only be one designation for all clergymen. That's why it says *chaplain* instead of *rabbi*. They added a Star of David to my jeep so that I wouldn't be stopped to perform last rites, but I've managed to do it a time or two anyway."

"So this is a Jewish army curate," Heinrich says, rather astonished. "But you two, you're going to have to put on more pitiful faces and look a little more miserable, if he's going to minister to your needs."

For us the war is over, but we have to wait until it is over for everyone. The days are getting longer, lovelier, and warmer. And on one of these days we suddenly hear a crazy honking noise, and then we see one of the black American boys behind the steering wheel of his truck with an equally crazy grin on his face. He has taped an issue of the army newspaper *Stars and Stripes* onto the windshield. There are only two words printed across the entire page. The closer his vehicle approaches, the larger and more legible the letters become: NAZIS QUIET.

Nearby there is a large concrete pool that had been built to hold water to fight the fires caused by falling bombs, but now it is empty and the U.S. boys are using it as a baseball diamond. They stop playing. The bats, the caps, and the mitts all fly into the air. The spectators, who had been sitting on the embankment, leap up, waving their arms in the air. Among them is a short black soldier with palms as pink as the paws of a bear cub, and he turns somersaults. One of the Puerto Ricans, whose unit is being quartered in the villa across the street from ours, is standing motionless with his head up against the wall. Freshly baked doughnuts are flying out of the canteen kitchen. An old man in street clothes pauses in his slow advance, leans forward on his cane, and looks around. We can't hear him, but we can see the question in his face: "So is the war finally over? On 8 May 1945?"

As soon as the sun sets, everyone rips the blackout shades out of the windows. Their own light will stream out into this new sky.

The heavens are being crisscrossed by searchlights. From beyond the Rhine one of them is sweeping back and forth across the sky, from one end to the other, with the regularity of a giant metronome, and I am fascinated. I know what the boy beyond the horizon is signaling to the whole world: "I will not be killed—I will not be slaughtered—I will live—love—live."

❧

Penance Accompanied by Bassoon

In the sixties, and into the first years of the seventies, two important Treblinka trials were held in the superior court in Düsseldorf. The Doll Franz, the Angel of Death Miete, along with a few others, were defendants in the first trial. The defendant in the second trial was Lord Stangl, who had been extradited from Brazil. He had been working at a Volkswagen plant in São Paolo. Supposedly there had been nothing in his personnel file. It was empty, blank. All three were sentenced to life imprisonment. Shortly after that, Stangl died in prison of a heart attack. Miete also died in prison. At the end of 1990 Franz was still alive behind bars.

Suchomel, among the gentlest of them, is supposed to have declared to the court: "Your honor, for all of these years, until my arrest, I have been playing bassoon in the church orchestra—without pay." Can the impact of a hand grenade really be so minimal? Back then, at the time of the uprising, he and his white uniform had disappeared from view in the clouds of an explosion. He died too, after spending six years in jail and then being released. Küttner had been wounded during the uprising but was never found. There were rumors that he had gone underground in the German Democratic Republic. He would only have to have changed his party registration, not his profession as a police chief. Fifty-four survivors of the Treblinka Uprising testified at both of these trials. They had survived in various ways. They came to the trials from their homes in many different countries. Fifty-four of eight hundred thousand? Nine hundred thousand? One million? I was a witness too. And during the entire trial I waited anxiously for the appearance of another kind of witness. To what is perhaps the greatest satisfaction I have ever known, that witness never came. Not a single one of them stood up, at attention, eyes forward, to declare: Yes, I did it out of a sense of conviction, I was then and still remain devoted to that ideal, and I am ready at any time to take responsibility for what I have done. Not a single one.

To my great disappointment, not one of the architects of the Treblinka camp was brought to the witness box, not one of the men who had hatched the plans, not one who had sketched in the outlines, not one who had worked out the details of construction, the insulation of the gas chambers—and, of course, not one who had "managed the whole operation from some distant, top-floor office."

The only brick building in camp, the one housing the gas chambers, was not destroyed during the uprising. Supposedly these chambers were used to end a few hundred more lives. In the fall of 1943 the whole camp was finally demolished, and Ukrainian peasant families were moved in to farm the land. They later fled, perhaps fearing the approaching Russians, or the spirits of the dead, or the living spirits who kept coming back at night to dig up gold and jewelry. Today an impressive monument is sitting on this site.

After Hitler's darkness, I returned to Czechoslovakia only to find myself struggling through Stalin's darkness. I consoled myself with the thought that this had not emanated from darker forces within my own country but had been imposed from the outside.

Having been judged a politically unreliable element, I was forced to do manual labor in a steel plant from 1951 until 1953. My fellow workers were more than a little surprised at how well this "pen pusher" could handle heavy drop hammers, glowing furnaces, and molten steel. Once the country began to make its way toward a political spring, my own situation also improved.

After the Prague Spring was crushed, I fled to Switzerland with my wife, my daughter, and my son. I said we had to come to a decision—the single-family house where my wife had grown up, the garden where our children played, to leave all of this—as if we were in danger of being deported in the next few days. Compared with my escape from Treblinka, this was a fine and dignified escape.

What happened to the diamonds with which Karl Unger and I survived, and which survived with us? There were two identical rings made with those diamonds. Jean, Karl's widow in the United States, is wearing one. My wife is wearing the other. Today you could probably begin telling the story of these rings with the words "Once upon a time, there was a place enclosed by a high green fence . . ."

❀

Jewish Lives

IDA FINK
A Scrap of Time and Other Stories

LISA FITTKO
Solidarity and Treason: Resistance and Exile, 1933–1940

RICHARD GLAZAR
Trap with a Green Fence: Survival in Treblinka

ARNOŠT LUSTIG
Children of the Holocaust